Praise for Ellen Evert Hopman

pRiestess of tHe foRest

A fascinating and romantic historical novel rooted in the author's deep knowledge of Celtic Druidism.

> —*Isaac Bonewits, Archdruid emeritus of Ár nDraíocht Féin*
> *(A Druid Fellowship) and author of* Neopagan Rites

From the very beginning, I was drawn into this story and found myself mesmerized by it. It is a tale which rings with sincerity, warmth, color, and depth.

> —*Philip Carr-Gomm, Chosen Chief of the Order of Bards,*
> *Ovates and Druids*

An authentically human tale of love, hope, and survival. Once I started reading, I was held captive until the very last page.

> —*Christopher A. LaFond, Druid harper and professor*
> *of languages, Boston College*

Wise women and clever men are in for a treat in this magnificent book, another thread in the re-weaving of our sacred wisdom.

> —*Susun Weed, wise woman, herbalist, and author of*
> Wise Woman Herbal for the Childbearing Year

A lively tale . . . While set in a richly imagined ancient Ireland, *Priestess of the Forest* offers an intriguing vision of a Druid path with lessons to teach the modern world.

> —*John Michael Greer, Grand ArchDruid, Ancient Order of Druids*
> *in America and author of* Encyclopedia of Natural Magic

This narrative is a beautiful glance back at pagan culture, Druidic practices and rituals, and daily Celtic life.

> —*Historical Novels Review*

This is a fast-moving story that quickly drew me [into] the world of Druidic Ireland.

—*ACTION, newsletter for the Alternate Religions Educational Network*

Hopman's ability to incorporate moving and beautiful examples of ritual into the narrative without too much disruption demonstrates a nascent talent for blending historical scholarship, modern practice, and individual inspiration into effective storytelling.

—*Bond of Druids: A Druid Journal*

[A] beautiful expression of [Ethne's] life drenched in the smells and songs of the herbs that are important to her craft.

—*The Druid Network, druidnetwork.org*

Characters are well developed and genuine … I highly recommend this book equally to readers who are new to the Celtic tradition as well as those who practice Druidism or related earth-based spirituality.

—*Inner Tapestry Holistic Journal*

A masterfully crafted tale that teaches as well as entertains.

—*Magicware Pagan Book Review, magickware.wordpress.com*

An edu-tainment treasure that I recommend for any Druid library.

—*Mike Gleason, Reformed Druids of North America*

Ellen Evert Hopman exudes throughout a sense of deep passion and true heart, with an earnest wish to rekindle the once great honour we had for our lands and each other.

—*Druidic Dawn, druidicdawn.org*

the Druid isLe

While Hopman's research and careful descriptions of Druid rituals, beliefs, and philosophy will be invaluable to those seeking the Druid path, she has succeeded in writing alive, compelling novels that will keep any reader turning page after page, far into the night.

> —*Patricia Lee Lewis, founder of Patchwork Farm Writing & Yoga Retreats and author of the award-winning book of poems* A Kind of Yellow

This daring sequel follows two intersecting stories of a young monk and a Druidess, one seeking to know his hidden origins, the other seeking to save her ancestral ways. Their journeys during the tumultuous historical setting of third-century Gaul, Britain, and Ireland will provide you with a series of wisdom lessons and insight into the clash of two worldviews. *The Druid Isle* is a must-have for any serious Druidic library.

> —*Michael Scharding, archivist of the Reformed Druids of North America and publisher of the* Druid Inquirer

Ellen has done it again with a wonderful sequel. The book grabs you right from the start … One of the best features is the small bits of old lore from the Druids scattered throughout. I would definitely recommend this book for anyone's library!

> —*Rev. Skip Ellison, Archdruid of Ár nDraíocht Féin (ADF) and author of* Ogham: The Secret Language of the Druids *and* The Solitary Druid: A Practitioner's Guide

aʙout tʜe autʜoʀ

Ellen Evert Hopman is a Master Herbalist and lay homeopath who holds an M.Ed. in mental health counseling. She is also a certified writing instructor. She was vice president of the Henge of Keltria, an international Druid fellowship, for nine years. She is the founder of the Whiteoak Internet mailing list, an online Druid ethics study group, and a co-founder of the Order of the Whiteoak (*Ord Na Darach Gile*). She is a current co-chief of the Order.

The
DRUID
ISLE

For Jeanne with the blessing of the Sea Realm!

ELLEN EVERT HOPMAN

Author of *Priestess of the Forest*

Ellen Evert Hopman

2019

Llewellyn Publications
Woodbury, Minnesota

FIRST EDITION
First Printing, 2010

Cover hooded woman photography by Ellen Dahl
Cover background © Digital Stock
Cover design by Ellen Dahl
Map on pages xxii–xxiii by Jared Blando

Llewellyn is a registered trademark of Llewellyn Worldwide, Ltd.

*Cover model used for illustrative purposes only
and may not endorse or represent the book's subject matter.*

*This is a work of fiction. Names, characters, places, and incidents are either the product
of the author's imagination or are used fictitiously, and any resemblance to actual persons,
living or dead, events, or locales is entirely coincidental.*

Library of Congress Cataloging-in-Publication Data
Hopman, Ellen Evert.
  The Druid Isle / Ellen Evert Hopman.—1st ed.
    p. cm.
  Includes bibliographical references and index.
  ISBN 978-0-7387-1956-6
  1. Druids and Druidism—Fiction. I. Title.
  PS3608.O6585D78 2010
  813'.6—dc22
                        2010001226

Llewellyn Publications
A Division of Llewellyn Worldwide, Ltd.
2143 Wooddale Drive
Woodbury, MN 55125-2989
www.llewellyn.com

Printed in the United States of America

OTHER BOOKS BY ELLEN EVERT HOPMAN

Tree Medicine, Tree Magic
(Phoenix Publishers)

A Druid's Herbal for the Sacred Earth Year
(Inner Traditions/Destiny Books)

Being a Pagan, with Lawrence Bond
(Inner Traditions/Destiny Books)

Walking the World in Wonder: A Children's Herbal
(Healing Arts Press)

Grimoire for the Apprentice Wizard
co-author with Oberon Zell Ravenheart
(New Page Books)

A Druid's Herbal of Sacred Tree Medicine
(Destiny Books)

Priestess of the Forest: A Druid Journey
(Llewellyn)

Three things that constitute a poet: knowledge that illumines, teinm laeda ("extempore recitation, illumination of song"), improvisation.
—*Ancient Irish triad*

contents

acknowledgments

Many thanks to Janet (Rowan) Scott, Sandy Barr, and Stan Stanfield of the Findhorn Community in Scotland for refreshing my memory of a trip taken over twenty years ago. Thanks to Mairi MacArthur for leads to early monastic communities, to Robert Jones for aerial photos of Iona, to Professor Michael O'Connell (Paleoenvironmental Research Unit, Department of Botany, National University of Ireland) for pollen studies that mention yew, to Donald Michael Craig, Donata Ahearn, Vyvyan Ogma Wyverne, and to Joyce Sweeny for help, advice, and support. Maureen Buchanan Jones deserves collaborative credit for her contribution to this book, and, as always, many thanks to Alexei Kondratiev for language assistance.

gLossaRy
anò
pRONUNCiatioN guiòe

adorare (Latin; ah-do-RAH-reh): to worship

Albu (Old Irish; ALL-uh-buh): Britain

ametis (Old Irish; AH-me-tish): amethyst

Ard-Ban-Drui (Old Irish; AHRD-VAHN-DREE): archdruidess

Ard-Drui (Old Irish; AHRD-DREE): archdruid

Ard-Ri (Old Irish; AHRD-REE): high king

Ard-Rigain (Old Irish; AHRD-REE-GAHN): high queen

Armorica (Old Irish; ar-MOH-ree-kah): Brittany

Asherah (Asherar-yam/Astarte—Syrian; AH-SHAIR-ah): Mother of
the Gods, Lady of the Sea, wife of El

auxilia (Latin; owk-SEE-lee-ah): additional troops, extra soldiers

Baal (Syrian; BAH-ahl): the Canaanite ruler god

ban-fili (Old Irish; BAHN-FILL-uh): a female sacred poet and diviner

ban-sidaige (Old Irish; BAHN-SHEE-thuh-hyuh): female fairy

beirel (Old Irish; BER-el): beryl

bell branch: a Druidic tool consisting of a branch with nine bells
affixed to it; depending on their rank, a Druid poet was entitled
carry one made of bronze, silver, or gold

Beltaine (Old Irish; BYEL-tin-yuh): May Day, the first day of
summer

bile (Old Irish; BILL-uh): sacred tree of a tribe or a district *bíle samrata (Old Irish; BILL-uh Sow-ruh-thuh):* sacred tree of summer

Brehon (Old Irish; BREH-ON): a lawyer and judge of the Druid caste, one who has memorized the ancient Brehon Laws

bríg (Old Irish; BREEGH): energy

Brighid (Old Irish; BREE-ghij): the great Triple Goddess of Smithcraft, Healing, and Poetry, who was the patroness of the Druids and bards

caldarium (Latin; kahl-DAH-ree-oom): hot bath

Caledonia (Latin; Kah-leh-DO-nee-ah): Scotland

Cantlos (Gaulish; KAHN-tloss): September/October "song month" (harvest, from the Coligny calendar[1])

carnyx (CAR-NIX): a wind instrument of the Iron Age Celts, a bronze trumpet

carreg (Cornish; CAR EGG): rocks

Cave canem (Latin; KAH-weh KAH-nem): "Beware of the dog"

centuria (Latin; ken-TOO-ree-ah): eighty men under a centurion

centurion (Latin; ken-TOO-ree-ohn): Roman commanding officer who leads a centuria

Chons da! (Cornish; Chons dah): "Good luck!"

Cinad ó muir (Old Irish; Kin-uth oh vwuir): "Judgment of the sea," where a criminal is placed in the ocean in a curach without any oars. If he survives, he becomes a person without status or protection on the shore upon which he lands.

commus (Old Irish; KOH-muhs): power

Compline (English): the night prayer, prayer at the end of the day

corann (Old Irish; KOR-un): crown

corma (Gaulish; KOR-mah): ale made with honeycombs

cornicer (Latin; Kor-nee-kair): horn blower

Cornubia (Latin; kor-NOO-bee-ah): Cornwall

cride (Old Irish; KREE-thuh): the heart

Cristaide, Cristaidi (pl.) (Old Irish; KREES-tih-thuh): Christian

cristall dub (Old Irish modern reconstruction; KRIS-tul DUV): dark crystal, smoky quartz, cairngorm

cristall glain (Old Irish modern reconstruction; KRIS-tul GLAHN): clear crystal

cristall grisainech (Old Irish modern reconstruction; KRIS-tul GRISS-AN-yukh): ruddy (rose) quartz

curach (Old Irish; KUR-ukh): a coracle, a small leather boat

curmi (Lepontic, possibly Gaulish; KOOR-mee): ale

daemones (Latin; DYE-mon-ess): demons

In Daghda (Old Irish; in DAWGH-thuh): "the Good God"; master of every art and patron of the Druids, he possessed an inexhaustible cauldron of plenty

Deo gratias (Latin; DEH-oh GRAH-tsyass): "Thanks be to God"

dessel (Old Irish; DYESH-ul): sunwise, clockwise

Dominus vobiscum (Latin; DOM-ee-nooss VOB-ees-koom): "God be with you"

Drui, Druid (pl.) (Old Irish; DREE or DRWEE): the learned class of Celtic society, comprised of priests, lawyers, judges, healers, and teachers of the children of the nobility and other functions

Druidecht (Old Irish; DREE-thekht or DRWEE-thekht): Druid magic, magic

dun (Old Irish; DOON): a fort or fortress

ecnae bratánech (Old Irish; Eg-nuh brah-dawn-ukh): salmon wisdom

ecnae nathairech (Old Irish; EG-nuh NAH-thur-ukh): serpent wisdom

Ego te absolvo (Latin; EH-go TEH ab-SOL-vo): "I forgive you"

EL (Syrian): the Father of the Gods, the kindly Creator of created things, husband of Ashera/Asherar-yam/Astarte

Emhain Abhlach (Old Irish; A-win AW-lukh): the Apple Isle

eques, equites (pl.) (Latin; EK-wee-tess): cavalry officers, knights

Eqvos (Latin; EH-KWOS): "Horse Month" from the Celto-Roman, Gaulish Coligny calendar

Ériu (Old Irish; AIR-uh): a collection of about 125 or more independent kingdoms that once comprised the island of Éire

Faunus (Latin; FOW-noos): the Roman name for Pan, God of the Flocks and Wild Places

fennid (Old Irish; FYEN-nith): a member of a *fian*

fennidi (Old Irish; FYEN-nee-thee): members of a *fian*

ferox (Latin; FAIR-ox): savage

féth (Old Irish; FEYTH): a magic mist, stillness

fian (Old Irish; FEE-un): a band of warrior-hunters

fiana (Old Irish; FEE-un-uh): bands of warrior-hunters

fidchell (Old Irish; FEETH-hyell): a chess-like game

fili (Old Irish; FILL-uh): a sacred poet and diviner

filidecht (Old Irish; FILL-ee-thekht): the craft of the sacred poet and diviner

fion (Old Irish; FEEN): wine imported from Gaul

flaith (Old Irish; FLAITH): nobles

fogo (Cornish; FO-goo): cave, a type of souteraine

frigidarium (Latin; frig-id-AH-ree-oom): cold bath

fúaimm (Old Irish; FOO-im): sound

Galli (Latin; GAHL-lee): Gauls, a Gaulish person

Gallia (Latin; GAHL-lea-ah): Gaul

Germania (Latin; gair-MAH-nee-ah): the territory of the Germanic tribes

Giamonios (Gaulish; gya-MON-yoss): Gaulish full moon festival of the start of summer, equivalent to Beltaine

Grian (Old Irish; GREE-UHN): the Sun Goddess

Hispania (Latin; hiss-PAH-nee-ah): Spain

Ictis Insula (Latin; IK-tiss IN-soo-lah): St. Michael's Mount

imbas (Old Irish; IM-mus): poetic inspiration, prophetic vision *imbas forosnai (Old Irish; IM-muss FOR-oss-nee):* "illumination between the hands" or "palm knowledge of enlightening"

immram (Old Irish; IM-rov): mystical voyage to the Otherworld

incantores (Latin; in-kahn-TOR-ess): spell-makers

Innis Ibrach (Old Irish; IN-nish EEW-rukh): the Isle of Yew

Innis nan Druidneach (Old Irish; IN-nish nun DRWITH-nyukh): the Druid Isle, also known as Innish Nun

Inissi Leuca (Gaulish; IN-iss-ee LEH-oo-kah): the Island of Light

In Medon (Old Irish; in mYETH-on): the Central Kingdom

Irardacht (Old Irish; IR-er-thakht): the Place of Eagles, the Northern Kingdom of the island

Is buide lemm frit (Old Irish; iss-BWITH-uh LYEM FRIJ): "Thank you"

Ísu (Old Irish; EEs-uh): Jesus

Kana'nim (Syrian; kah-nah-NEEM): Canaanite people

laconium (Latin; lah-KON-ee-oom): a dry sauna

Lauds (English): the dawn prayer

legatus legionis (Latin; Leh-GAH-tooss leh-gee-OH-niss): the commander of a legion, appointed by the emperor usually for a three- to four-year term; also provincial governor

Letha (Old Irish; LYETH-uh): Gaul

liaig (Old Irish; LEE-igh): a Druid healer specializing in herbal healing, surgery, and magic

lingua franca (Latin; Ling-ooah frank-ah): an international auxiliary language used as common jargon between peoples

Loch Feabhail (Old Irish; LOKH FYEW-il): Loch Foyle

lorica musculata (Latin; LOR-ee-kah moos-koo-LAH-tah): a bronze chest piece made of two sections, one worn on the chest and one worn on the back, buckled at the sides; it was usually decorated with animal or mythological images, or exaggerated chest muscles

Lugnasad (Old Irish; LOO(gh)-nuss-uth): First Fruits; the pre-harvest festival celebrated during the first few weeks of August

lupa (Latin; LOO-pah): she-wolf

Mamm an Bys (Cornish; Mahm an Beez): Earth Mother, Mother of the World

Mannanán mac Lir (Old Irish; MAN-AH-NAN MOK LEER): God of the Sea

mantra (Sanskrit; MAHN-trah): a seed syllable or word used to focus the mind during meditation

Marah (Syrian; MAR-ah): merciful Goddess of the Waters

Mar plek (Cornish): "Please"

medu (Gaulish; MEH-doo): mead

Meur ras ta (Cornish; MER RAHSS tah): "Thank you"

mian (Old Irish; MEE-un): desire

mid (Old Irish; MEETH): mead

milites (Latin; MEE-lee-tess): foot soldiers (also, milites Gregarius)

Mithras (MYTH-rass): a God of Light, Truth, and the Sun, favored by Roman soldiers

Nantosuelta (Gaulish; NAHN-to-SWEL-tah): "Winding River," a Gaulish deity

Nemed (Old Irish; NEH-MED): sacred, the highest caste of society, including the Druid and ruling aristocrats

nemed (Old Irish; NEH-veth): a sacred enclosure

Nemetona (NEH-MEH-TOE-NAH): female spirit of the sacred grove

numen (Latin; NOO-men): divine power, or spirit

Ogum (Old Irish; Oh-gum): the ancient Celtic alphabet and script

Paganus, Pagani (pl.) (Latin; PAH-GAH-NEE): Pagans, non-Christians, literally "country dwellers," ones who worship the Old Gods

palaestra (Latin; pah-LICE-trah): an outdoor gym

Pater Noster (Latin; PAH-tair NOSS-tair): Our Father

peplos (Greek; PEP-loss): a lady's garment made with two rectangles of cloth, fastened with two large pins at the shoulders and folded over at the top in both front and back

Prime (English): early morning (usually about 6 AM) prayers

pulla (Latin; pull-lah): a shawl worn by a married woman to cover her head

quern (English; KERN): two millstones laid on top of each other to grind grain

rath (Old Irish; RAHTH): earthen rampart, a ring-fort

rígain (Old Irish; REE-ghun): queen

Romanus, Romani (pl.) (Latin, also Gaulish; Ro-MAH-nee): Romans

saidecht (Old Irish; SWEE-thekht): mastery

sally rods: willow branches used for thatching

Samain (SAV-in [mediaeval] SOW-in [modern]): the Celtic New Year, the start of winter (Halloween)

scatho (Cornish; SCATHO): boat

schola (Latin; SKO-lah): school

shillelagh (Irish; SHIL-LEY-LEE): a club-like weapon

siabainn (Old Irish; SHE-vin): soap

sidhe (Irish; SHEE-thuh [mediaeval] SHEE [modern]): the fairies

signifier (Latin; SIG-nee-fair): accountant and pay master for a Roman centurion, also the standard bearer who carries the centurial signum; a spear shaft with an open hand, signifying loyalty

sith (SHEETH): peace

Sol Invictus (Latin; SOL in-WIK-tooss): Apollo, the great Sun God

solus (Old Irish; SOL-uss): light

Sucellos (Gaulish; Soo-KEL-loss): "the Good Striker," a Gaulish deity

súil inmedónach (Old Irish; SOOL in-veth-AWN-ukh): the inner eye

tech ind allais (Old Irish; TYEKH in ALL-ish): sweat house

teinm laegda (Old Irish; TYEN-um LWEEGH-thuh): "extempore recitation, illumination of song"

tepidarium (Latin; the-pid-AH-ree-oom): warm, tepid bath

theron (Greek; Theh-ron): hunter

tigris (Latin; TEEG-riss): tigress

tirones (Latin; tee-ROAN-ess): raw or new recruits, soldiers in training

torc (TORC): a Celtic neck ring symbolic of noble status

Torcrad (TORK-ruth): the Kingdom of the South, the People of the Boar

triskell, triskellean (pl.); (TRIS-KEL): a design consisting of three spirals rotating out of a common center, representing the three worlds of land, sea, and sky

tuath (Old Irish; TOO-uth): country district, tribal area

tuathamail (Old Irish; TOOTH-uh-vul): earthwise, counterclockwise

turcait (Old Irish; TUR-kij): turquoise

uinom (Lepontic; WEEN-om): wine

vallum (Latin; WAL-loom): earthworks

vellum (Latin; WELL-oom): a sheet of skin prepared for writing

Vesta (Latin; WES-tah): Roman Goddess of the Hearth

Villa Candida (Latin; WIL-lah KAHN-dee-dah): the White Villa

Villa Rustica (Latin; WIL-lah ROOS-tee-kah): farmhouse, rustic villa

vinum (Latin; WEE-noom): wine

Waters of Life: whiskey, from Old Irish *uisce,* "water," and *bethad,* "of life," meaning literally "water of life"

the characters

Aífe (AHY-FAH): a young woman in training to become a Druid

Albinus (AL-BEE-NUHS): a Roman monk

Amalgáid (AH-vul-ghawth): a Drui from Innis nan Druidneach

Anna: grandmother of Aurelia

Brother Armel: a member of the Inissi Leuca community of monks

Asbolos (Latin): "soot," a slave in Decimus and Flavia's house

Aude: Aurelia's aunt

Aurelia: a young woman from the mainland of Armorica

Báetán (BWEE-dawn): a Drui from Innis nan Druidneach

Bébinn (BEY-vin): a Ban-Drui from Innis nan Druidneach

Breaca: sister of Aurelia

Cadfan (KAHD-vahn): grandfather of Aurelia

Cadla: king of In Medon, the central kingdom

Cathail: son of Clothru and Damán

Cináed: king of Irardacht

Cuill: son of Clothru and Damán

Clothru (KLOTH-ruh): a female apprentice Druid

Coemgen (KWEEV-ghyen): the former Ard-Drui of the island

Crimthann (KRIV-thun): former high king of the central kingdom,
   In Medon, and of the island

Daire (DAR-yuh): a prince, son of the former high king Crimthann

Dáiríne (DAWR-in-yuh): a Ban-Drui from Innis nan Druidneach

Damán (DAV-awn): a male apprentice Druid

Decimus Servius Tiberius (DECK-ee-mooss SAIR-vyoos tib-AIR-ee-ooss): legatus legionis for the province of Aquitania

Denzil: son of Hammitt

Elowen: daughter of Hammitt

Eseld: daughter of Hammitt

Eógan (YO-ghun): son of Cadla, king of In Medon

Ethne (ETH-nuh): the archdruidess of the Forest School and an herbal healer

Flavia Prima (FLAH-vee-ah PREE-mah): wife of Decimus Servius Tiberius

Gaine (GAN-yuh): an elderly archdruidess

Gaine Óg (GAN-yuh AWG; "little Gaine"): daughter of Clothru and Damán

Gaius Quintus Aurelius (GUY-ooss KWIN-tooss OW-RAIL-yoos): a centurion in Aquitania

Germanus (gair-MAH-nooss): an abbott from the island

Gnóe (Old Irish; gnwee): "beautiful, exquisite;" a cow

Gwen: sister of Teilo, member of a family of fisher folk

Hammitt: head man of the people of Dor Dama

Ienipa: wife of Hammitt

Isidore: companion to Martinus

Brother Justan: a boy novice from Inissi Leuca

Karenza: second wife of Hammitt

Brother Lucius: a child discovered amongst the fisher folk of Armorica

Máel Ísu (MWEEL EES-uh): a monk, Cadla's spiritual advisor

Martinus (mar-TEE-nooss): a traveling monk

Melor (MELL-or): Aurelia's father

Meraud: the ancient wise woman of the people of Dor Dama

Merryn: son of Hammitt

Abbott Mihael: abbott of the Armorican monastery at Inissi Leuca

Nárbflaith (NAWR-uv-lath): queen of In Medon and wife of Cadla

Nuin (Nin): a Drui living in the *nemed* of the Ard-Ri

Rochad (ROKH-uth): high king of Torcrad

Ruadh (ROO-uth): "red, wild, fierce one;" former member of the *fian*, now partner of Ethne

Ruadhán (ROO-uth-awn): son of Ethne and Ruadh

Sadwrn (SAH-doorn): Aurelia's uncle

Steren (STAIR-en): daughter of Hammitt

Tanaide (THAN-ih-thuh): son of Cadla, king of In Medon

Tannin (tah-NEEN): a Syrian slave

Brother Teilo (TILE-o): a boy novice from Inissi Leuca, from a family of fisher folk

Brother Trillo: a member of the Inissi Leuca community, caretaker of boys

Ugar (oo-gahr): a Syrian slave

Weluela: mother of Aurelia

Innis nan Druidneach
(Innis Ibrach)

Irardacht

Ériu

Murthracht

In Medon   Oirthir

The Forest
House

Torcrad

Albu
(Brittania)

Kernow
(Cornubia)

North Atlantic
drift

prevailing winds
in summer

Ictis Insula

Gulf Stream

Inissi
Leuca

Caledonia

Germania

rmorica

Letha
(Gallia)

Fourth-Century Celtic Western Europe

I am a wave on the windy sea
Over land and sea I am the wind
I am the eagle on the cliff
I am the stone within the mountain
I am the salmon in the forest pool
I am the strength of the boar in rut
I am the tines of the mountain stag
I am the bravery of the wild bull
I am the flower in bloom
I am the seed within the flower
I am the grain that feeds the people.

I am a word of magic
I am the strength within the strong
I am the silence within the secret
I am the knowledge within the knower
I am the enchanted point of a battle spear
I am the radiant sun of light
I am the stars in the cauldron of sky
I am the ages of the moon.

My word brings the world into being
I grow the shady wood
I release the cleansing waterfall
I hold the pool of the lake
I raise the lofty green meadow
I am the well in the hill
That nourishes the people
I am the people
I am the past
I am the future
I am the sacred land
I am the sea and the sky…

—Based on a poem by the bard Amairgen Glúingeal

pROLOGUE

It had rained for an entire moon-tide. The small stream was spilling its banks, the reedy shore laid flat by the weight of constant downpours. But at last the sun was shining. The children rushed out of doors as soon as breakfast was over, pulled equally by the warm sunlight and the exciting prospect of puddles.

Ethne carried wooden bowls and cups from the morning meal in a large willow basket, to clean them in the surging waters. As she plucked rushes for scouring, she reflected on what she and Ruadh had created together in the wilderness. She was older now, and crouching on the muddy bank to clean cups and dishes was becoming hard on her knees, but she still enjoyed seeing to the details of daily life in the Forest School. Her every waking moment was spent in passing on and preserving the ancient teachings, as much for the benefit of future generations as to honor those who had gone before. The Druid might no longer hold the status they once did, but at least Ethne could be sure she was doing everything in her power to preserve the ancient ways. She was satisfied that her life was fulfilling its purpose.

When the dishes were scrubbed, rinsed, and stacked neatly in the basket to dry, Ethne clapped her hands to get the children's attention.

"Who wants to take a walk and look for a day sign?"

"We do!" came the chorused answer from stained, muddy faces.

Walking out in search of a day sign was a favorite activity of the youngest students, because once they saw something significant—a raven, a deer, a pool, a rainbow, or any other natural feature that called attention to itself—Ethne would weave them a story.

On this day, they trooped towards a small river that wound its way through the forest. The rains had left it murky and swollen, and it was hard to calculate the depth of the waters.

"Let's sit by the riverbank and see what creature or object calls our attention," Ethne said.

The children arranged themselves around her like a tribe of goslings nestling against their mother and, Druid-trained, kept their silence. Ethne had taught them that to experience nature directly is the quickest and surest way to discover truth, for nature cares not what a person's station in life might be, nor for wealth and possessions. Nature cares little if one is pauper or king, male or female. Nature just is, and until you can see something reflected in nature, it simply isn't true.

Suddenly the silence was broken by a bright flash and a slap of water, then by rings of ripples edging towards shore. A moment later, there was a second flash and another arc of silver against the sunlight.

"It's the salmon!" the children shrieked.

"The salmon of wisdom," Ethne corrected, smiling. "See how they leap with ease between the worlds?"

She knew that after a long rain, the appearance of sun would bring out the flies and midges, and that the salmon would emerge, leaping for their breakfast. It was the perfect opportunity for a teaching tale.

"Deep beneath the ocean, there is a sacred well that is the source of all wisdom. It is known as the Well of Segais. Around it grow nine magical hazel trees that bear purple nuts. There are five magical salmon that live in that well, and as you know, salmon is the oldest creature on the face of the earth, the first to be created and thus the closest to the Source of life.

"Every time a purple hazelnut falls into the well, one of the five salmon leaps to catch it, and every time they swallow a nut, they grow a spot; by now the salmon must be covered with many spots, because those fish are very old."

"Why do they keep eating those nuts?" asked Cathail.

"Because they want to be wise," Ethne answered. "We Druid are just like the salmon. The hazelnuts represent knowledge, and each time a salmon swallows a nut, she becomes wiser. We too seek the sweetness that is hidden within the hard shell of learning, and when we have developed our wisdom and perfected our five senses, we learn to do as the salmon do and find our way back to the Source, to the waters of our birth."

"I like to eat the salmon," said Gaine Óg.

"Yes, so do I. Maybe if we ask nicely, Ruadh and Damán will build a weir and catch a few for our supper," Ethne answered, picking herself up from the damp grass to lead her charges back to the settlement, hidden deep in the forest.

part one

The Isle of Light

1

Lucius, Teilo, and Justan had discussed for months how to escape the island by boat and make it to the mainland for the big Giamonios festival. Blond-haired, blue-eyed Lucius was the natural leader of the pack, which was nicknamed "the triumverate" by the older brothers. Genial and daring, he was the one who most often slid into the kitchens at night to pilfer bread, cheese, and honey for the boys in the dormitory. Sometimes he even managed to smuggle out a whole goatskin of *vinum*, which the boys then passed around in their secret gathering place behind a thicket of trees.

The monks suspected that the boys were responsible for the sudden shortfalls in the kitchen stores but declined to make a fuss, thinking a silent tongue a virtue. When there was no longer enough bread and cheese to go around, Abbott Mihael would simply declare a day of fasting, a subtle but effective punishment for the boys.

Lucius excelled at his studies and had already memorized whole biblical chapters, to the delight of Abbott Mihael.

Teilo had dark brown curls and a faintly sprouting moustache, of which he was inordinately proud. He sprang from one of the fisher families from across the bay and had intimate knowledge of the rocks, shoals, and sandbars between Inissi Leuca and the mainland. Where Lucius was quick and bright, Teilo was strong and could be counted on to lift a body high into a tree or over a wall to snatch apples or grapes.

Abbott Mihael despaired of the boy ever perfecting his reading or his letters.

Justan, youngest of the three, idolized both Lucius and Teilo and followed their every command. With dark blond hair and moss-green eyes, he was self-effacing and quiet, shy and gentle as a deer. He rarely spoke unless addressed first.

Like Lucius, Justan had been placed at the monastery as an infant when his father died and his mother could no longer afford to keep him. He felt to the depths of his soul that his mother must have found him unlovable, else why would she have given him up so easily? When he spoke in the *schola*, it was usually to bring up a philosophical point upon which he had ruminated for days.

Unlike Lucius, Justan lacked self-confidence, and while he also lacked the physical vigor of Teilo, he did have quick and dexterous fingers. Abbott Mihael thought he might make a fine scribe one day and even suspected genius in the boy, but despaired how to pry it out of him.

After Vespers, the three engaged in one last game with a wool-filled leather ball until Brother Trillo was ordered by the abbott to shepherd the boys into the dormitory; *"Omnes ergo in unum positi compleant!* Since everyone is gathered, let them say Compline, the last prayer of the day,"* he directed in Latin. He was always seeking ways to further their erudition.

The days were growing longer, and it was becoming ever harder to corral them into their beds.

After Brother Trillo heard their bedtime prayers, blew out the candle, and left, the boys scrabbled under their straw mattresses and dug out the tunics and pants they had secreted away over time. They couldn't be seen in town wearing their brown wool scholar's robes, so Teilo's sister Gwen had given him a piece of clothing each time he went home for a visit. Teilo shared these with his friends. They had also done small favors for the monks and visitors to the island, and over many months had each successfully hoarded a pocketful of coins for food and drink in the town.

That night the moon was nearly full, so the boys knew that the Gia-monios festival would begin the very next day. After midnight, when the rest of the monastery was deep in slumber, they crept from the dormitory. To avoid the guard at the gate, they clambered over the old earthen *vallum* that surrounded the inner grounds to shelter the monks from the sea winds. Once free of that barrier, they walked around to the landward side of the island in the clear moonlight as quietly as they were able and edged along the beach to find a particular clump of greenery. They pulled a small leather curach from under the bushes where Teilo kept it hidden and carried it to the shoreline, hoisted up their trousers, and waded into the brine. Squeezing themselves into the shaky craft and drawing up their knees, they found themselves in a position where it was very difficult to paddle.

"Good thing the sea is calm tonight, or we would never make it over," said Teilo in a hoarse whisper. He cast an expert eye on the small, chopping waves.

"We can do it!" said Lucius out loud, with his usual optimism, caus-ing Teilo to shush him disapprovingly.

Justan said nothing but peered nervously at the sky, clutching the frame of the coracle. He was terrified of storms.

At length, they made it to the other side of the bay, dragged the small craft ashore, and lifted it over their heads to carry it to a clutch of large rocks well above the tide line. They rolled it upside down, hid the oars underneath, and covered the whole with seaweed to disguise it from thieves.

"I'm freezing!" said Teilo. Justan too was shivering, his lips already turning blue.

"We forgot to bring cloaks!" said Lucius with a slight feeling of panic.

"Well, we could dig a hole and pull the curach upside down over our heads. At least we would be out of the wind," said Justan.

It was a brilliant suggestion, all the more startling because of its source. They immediately set to work digging a hole in the sand, and finally, after pulling the craft overhead, curled together like puppies for a few hours of sleep.

The next morning, emerging turtle-like from the damp leather shell, they were horrified to see that the sky had clouded over. The sea had only a slight chop, but a steady breeze from the ocean, plus the sight of sea birds heading to shore, told them that a squall was coming.

"We have to go back now!" said Teilo.

"Yes, let's go right now!" echoed Justan.

Lucius considered their predicament. "No, I've been waiting years for this chance; I'm not going back. You can if you want to, but I'm staying here."

"You *can't* stay. How will you get back? And what will we tell Abbott Mihael?" Teilo argued. Justan shook his head.

"I can't go back. Not yet." Lucius's words were determined. "If you go back now, no one will even know that you left. Tell them you don't know what happened to me." He looked from one to the other. "It won't be a complete lie." He gave them his lopsided smile, the one that said he was way beyond them. It was the smile that had convinced them before, and they had never been sorry.

Teilo and Justan looked at each other, and then back at Lucius once more. Reluctantly, but with a growing sense of urgency, they went for the leather boat, hoisting it on their shoulders and making for the sea.

"I'll be all right!" yelled Lucius, waving towards the departing craft as it breached the swelling waves. The wind was already so strong that the departing two-thirds of the triumverate did not even hear him.

2

Lucius had never been off the island alone and anticipated the adventure with both pride and fear. He knew that he would be punished when he went back to Inissi Leuca, but to take part in the famous Festival of Summer was worth the price. He had heard tantalizing bits about this spectacle for years, and now he finally had the chance to see for himself why the brothers were forbidden to attend.

He had no idea where to go for food or shelter. He had no kin on the mainland. All he had been told was that he had been brought to the monastery as a baby by a pious tribe of fisher folk who had vowed to have a saint in the family—at least that was the story Abbott Mihael had told him. He often wondered why his family had taken no further interest in him, but each time he broached the subject, he was rebuffed. Even Brother Trillo avoided the subject, so he gradually gave up asking.

In the back of his mind was a recurring fantasy. What if he met a family on the mainland that looked just like him? Surely they would recognize him as one of their own, and he would know them too. He rarely spoke to anyone of the nagging hurt he carried, the longing for family and tribe. Abbot Mihael said the church and the monks and brothers were his tribe now, but it just wasn't enough; he wanted badly to be bound to someone, somewhere, as blood kin.

Now he was completely alone. He would have to trust in God to protect him, for didn't God care for even the lowly sparrow? "Lord, I am but a storm-crossed pilgrim; lead me to calm waters," he said reflexively, uttering a line from the old prayer to reassure himself.

A sudden pelt of cold rain splattered on his neck, and he quickly scrabbled up the dunes in search of any kind of shelter. When he reached the crest of a tall sand hill, he was astonished by what he saw; stretching into the distance as far as he could see was a vast tent city. Leather and cloth tarps and skins draped over poles made a sea of white and brown, with smoky cooking fires everywhere in between. He had never dreamed there could be so many people in one place. The tiny seaside village was dwarfed by the mushrooming splay of humanity.

Rain came in earnest now, and all he could think to do was beg for refuge in one of the outlying tents. He sprinted between tufts of sea grass and wild roses to the nearest one and called out a greeting: "In the name of God, may I come in and shelter from the rain?"

A pair of green eyes and a cascade of flaxen hair peered out of the dark tent, looked him up and down, and answered calmly, "You'll catch your death out there; come on in."

He pushed aside the leather flap and found no one inside but the young woman who had welcomed him.

"Where are you camping? Did you get lost?" she asked.

"Um, no, I am not camping. I came over for the day from across the bay. I wasn't expecting bad weather."

"I am called Aurelia. My family is from the peninsula. We have a goat farm," she said, proffering her outstretched hand in greeting.

"I am Lucius, from Inissi Leuca."

Her eyes widened, and she stepped back. "You're a monk...from the island?"

"Oh, no, I am just a laybrother, a student in the *schola*, actually."

"Well, what in the name of the gods are you doing here, on this day of all days? I thought your sort avoided our gatherings!"

"I have never been to one of your, um, gatherings before." His ears turned a deep shade of pink, and he found it very hard to meet her eyes. He had rarely seen a female this close, let alone spoken to one. Now that he was actually alone with one, it was most unnerving.

"I can show you around once the rains stop," she offered.

She eyed him closely, speculating. His thick, long hair and blue eyes were quite becoming, and she could tell that he had no idea how handsome he was. She was beginning to enjoy the chance encounter.

"My parents went to my grandparents' tent to make arrangements for the feast. They must have been caught in the bad weather, just like you. Would you like to share a cup of *uinom* while we wait for the storm to pass?"

"You have *uinom*? On Inissi Leuca, that is a drink only for special occasions and for Mass," he said with a guilty twinge. He decided not to reveal his late-night pilfering in the monastery kitchens, lest he lose face in her eyes.

"Oh, yes. One of the main points of festival week is to share *uinom*, *curmi*, *medu*, and other such drinks with all you meet—friends, strangers, everyone!"

Her eyes twinkled as she took down a goatskin bag hanging from a tent pole, uncorked it, and squeezed a stream of ruby liquid into a little clay cup. Her expression revealed a joyful sense of anticipation.

This year's festival is going to be fun, she thought, smiling and handing a brimming cupful to the handsome stranger and pouring another for herself.

3

"Damnation and perdition, Brother Trillo! How could you let this happen?" Abbott Mihael was almost beyond words in his disbelief.

Teilo and Justan had returned safely but not without notice, and were immediately sent to separate cells to remain in solitary reflection and confinement for a week. Their single daily meal was to be water and oatmeal gruel into which ashes had been mixed. Abbott Mihael glared as the monks and brothers seated themselves at the long wooden dining table in the Great House.

"This is the worst possible time to lose Lucius!" Mihael continued. "That wretched Martinus has threatened for months to come here at the time of the Giamonios festival. He wants to disrupt it just like the Cristos punished the money changers at the temple in Jerusalem. He imagines that he and Isidore can simply charge between the stalls and knock them all down, and that the *Pagani* will sit still for it, meek as a flock of ewes!

"I can't *stand* the sight of Martinus. He is ugly and cruel, his clothing is filthy, and his hair is disgusting! He fancies himself some kind of Old Testament prophet. Now I'm hearing stories from the mainland that he is so holy, he can even raise the dead!"

Abbott Mihael paced the floor. He suspected that a cult was developing around the repulsive monk and his troops, for what else could they be called? His followers roamed the countryside of Gallia like any Roman auxiliary, smashing shrines, tearing temples apart stone by stone, and cutting down the sacred groves and trees of the *Pagani*.

"Ye shall destroy their altars, break their images, and cut down their groves … for the Lord, whose name is jealous, is a jealous God," was one of Martinus's favorite quotations from Exodus. The type of men who surrounded Martinus did nothing to enhance the monk's image, as far as the abbott was concerned. Most were failures, unable to woo a woman, raise a family successfully, or maintain a farm. In their bitterness, they exulted in the vicarious power and feeling of accomplishment that Martinus gave them.

Unbelievably, he had the full backing of Rome. There were even rumors that he was to be made a bishop! There was little Mihael could do to prevent his comings and goings from Inissi Leuca, and he feared that Martinus might find converts among the brothers.

"I wish everyone to stay silent on this subject for as long as possible," Mihael ordered. "The two boys are safely hidden in their cells, and there is no reason to let on that we have lost one of them. Tell Martinus, if he asks, that they are being kept in solitary confinement for a boyish infraction and are not to see daylight for a week.

"Brother Armel, go to the guesthouse and prepare it for Martinus and Isidore's visit. As for the rest of you, let us ring the bell for Vespers and contemplate on how we are all sinners, in dire need of grace."

Martinus arrived the next morning, his appearance coinciding with the Giamonios festival, as expected. He wore a hair shirt under his robes and smelled as if he had not washed for weeks. His companion, Isidore, was in the same condition. Abbott Mihael saw lice in their hair and made a mental note to have Brother Armel burn their mattresses and boil their sheets in seawater after they left. Martinus would not accept food or hospitality on arrival; instead, he rang the bell to call the community to prayer in the wooden chapel. He had an urgent message to impart.

"All dancing shall be forbidden on the mainland!" he cried out even before all were assembled. "It invites wantonness, and the women move too freely. The men make lustful glances when the *Pagani* dance in their so-called temples and shrines! There shall be no moving or stamping of feet and no waving of hands! There shall be no wreathed dancers and no hand clapping to music!

"I know that some of you priests allow dancing as long as it is part of a Christian worship service. This is forbidden! There is no such thing as 'spiritual dance.' The men thrust themselves around and the women show their ankles and shins while they let their hair fall loose. It invites sex! It is Satanic!" He railed on and on until flecks of spit flew from his mouth onto the monks and brothers.

"There is no such thing as Pagan worship! *Adorare* is a word that only applies to Christians and the Christian God! The Pagans are deluded by the *daemones* that they call gods. They are deviants, heretics; their so-called rites are a calumny against all that is holy!

"Nor shall they sing. The only sacred singing is to chant the psalms. It is the only singing permissible. The *Pagani* sing songs of love and lust all night at their feasts. They even sing to their demon gods in their temples!"

Martinus was panting now. Isidore rushed to hand him a cup of water, which he accepted. Too overcome by emotion to speak, he raised his battered copy of the Bible and held it aloft, pointing to it. "Amen!" he uttered as Isidore took his elbow and guided him from the chapel to the guesthouse.

4

The rain ended and warm sunlight glistened on the soaked tents as the Giamonios camp came slowly back to life. Mothers emerged from their hide-and-cloth shelters to relight the dampened cooking fires, and children screamed with delight, hopping in and out of the puddles that had welled up in the pathways.

Aurelia parted the hide door of her family's tent, sniffing the moist, earthy air. The sound of a cowbell drew closer from the far end of the path, and she grabbed for Lucius's hand.

"Come, look! It's an ox for the sacrifice!"

A huge white bull trudged up the muddy path at a dignified pace. Beautifully washed and curried, it sported a garland of flowers and grasses around its massive neck. Braided strings of wildflowers twined its long horns, and colorful ribbons were plaited into its silky tail. A knot of people followed the beast, among them the family that was sponsoring the sacrificial offering, singing a song inviting the people and the gods to join the party.

As the bull lumbered by the open flaps of the tent, Lucius was startled to see bold writing along the sides of the huge beast. The family offering the animal had written their name in large, oily, red ochre letters for all to see. Lucius wondered how many, other than perhaps the tribal leaders, would be able to read the advertisement.

Stepping into the strengthening sunlight, Lucius and Aurelia picked their way gingerly to avoid the worst of the mud and occasional animal droppings, and Lucius took in for the first time the breadth of humanity at the gathering. He was amazed by the wealth of colors the people wore—deep reds and blues, greens and yellows; a riot of color to the eyes of one used to the quiet whites and browns of the brothers' robes. Men, women, and children sported wreaths of fresh greenery, ribbons, and flowers on their heads.

There was music everywhere, groups of musicians appeared quickly after the storm, clustered together in front of their tents to sing hymns to the sun or play lyres, cymbals, flutes, and drums. And there was dancing. Lines of dancers held hands and wended barefoot along the paths, urging festivalgoers to join them. To Lucius, it was all new and exciting; he had never dreamed so many people could be made so happy all at once.

Moving closer to the center of the teeming crowd, they approached a sacred precinct of sorts. Elders, priests, and priestesses had set up tables and altars under the trees, which were garlanded with ribbons and wind chimes in honor of the celebration. Some were casting lots with dice or sheep bones, offering to divine the future for a small price. Merchants displayed tiny oil lamps and beeswax candles for ritual use, and there were moon-shaped sacrificial cakes for sale, to offer to the ritual fires or to take home for luck. For those who could afford them, there were glass and silver cups, along with silver strainers and wine dippers with "To the god Faunus" inscribed on the side. Herbalists with their fresh-cut medicinal herbs and salves plied their wares, and *incantores* offered charms against fever as well as little goddess statues to promote fertility in women.

A group of male worshippers shouldered a statue of a goddess on a wooden pallet and paraded her around the central area, moving her in a wide circle for all to see. A line of priestesses followed the men, singing her praises. The wooden statue was lightly painted in gold leaf and festooned with fresh flowers. People reached out to touch her for luck or to offer a small blossom of their own in her honor. A large red cloth tent marked the exact center of the ritual precinct.

"What goes on in there?" Lucius asked, wide-eyed.

"It's the shrine of the Goddess and the God of this festival. Shall we go in and pay homage?" Aurelia asked.

Lucius was suddenly afraid. All of his training since early childhood had told him to avoid the "Satanic revels" of the *Pagani*, and yet here he was, about to enter a red tent that was the very color of hell fire. His heart shrank in fear at the prospect of what he might find within. Would it cause him to lose his soul or be damned for all eternity? He froze, unable to will his limbs to move.

"What is the matter with you? You look like someone who has had a bad shock."

"I … I need to know what is inside that tent before I set foot in there. I need to know what will happen to me."

Aurelia sensed real terror in him. She was not surprised, knowing that he was a *Cristaide* from Inissi Leuca.

"I don't know what your priests have told you about our beliefs, but no hurt will come to you from anyone at this festival or from those inside the tent. Among us, it is considered great good fortune to attend this gathering. Everyone is welcome here to receive the blessing of the gods. Inside the tent are the living representatives of the God and Goddess of this festival. I promise you, you will come to no harm!"

He did not want to look like a coward, especially in front of this girl. His feelings when he looked at her confused him. He rather liked the confusion. He offered up a silent prayer of protection to the archangel Michael:

Sancte Michael Archangele, defende nos in proelio,
contra nequitiam et insidias diaboli esto praesidium …

Thus shielded, he found the courage to continue. "Well, I have come this far; I may as well see what's in there," he said.

They moved together to join the long line of people snaking into the red tent. As they waited their turn, Aurelia noticed that others, especially the younger women, were staring appreciatively at Lucius. She felt proud that the tall blond stranger was at her side.

Lucius noticed that the worshippers bore gifts: a small coin, a pinch of incense for the altar, a recently purchased candle or oil lamp, fruits, bread, or flowers from the fields surrounding the encampment. He reached into his pocket and held out his coins.

"What is the appropriate offering?" he asked.

"The gods recognize good intentions. A small copper will be enough for both of us. Drop it into the little wooden box by the door when we go in, or you can hand it to the God himself when you greet him."

"What do you mean? Will the God be there to meet us in person?" He felt a little like he was drowning and had to remember to take a breath.

"Of course he will. That's the whole point! You'll see."

When their turn came to enter, it took a moment for Lucius's eyes to adjust to the murky interior. Candles and oil lamps twinkled all around the perimeter of the huge tent and also on small tables and altars. The air was thick with incense; a woman clad in a very thin toga wafted smoke towards those who entered, using a white dove's wing. Lucius startled and blinked, then turned deep red. He could see the woman's breasts and private parts through the gauzy cloth, and he pried his eyes away with difficulty. He was foundering, lost in unfamiliar images and sensations and the involuntary reactions of his own body. An unexpected firmness blossomed between his legs, and he was suddenly very glad that his tunic stretched almost to his knees.

Two large wooden thrones stood back to back in the center of the tent. Aurelia clutched his hand tightly and pulled him forward to stand directly before one of them, upon which a long-haired woman sat in languid pose, clothed in green and red garments with a thick golden torc around her neck. She had a tall, loosely woven wicker cage filled with white doves to one side of her and an enormous wicker cage filled with ravens on the other. A beautifully woven rug and a wide, shallow, earthenware dish of water lay at her feet.

"What is your wish, my son?" she asked dreamily.

Lucius thought she had drunk too much *vinum* or maybe she was in some kind of trance. His mind went blank in panic, and Aurelia nudged his side sharply.

"Ask for a prophecy!" she hissed into his ear.

This was a terrible sin! The only prophecy allowed on Inissi Leuca was to open a Bible at random and interpret the passage upon which your finger happened to land. Before he could utter a sound, the woman on the throne turned her hooded eyes to him and began to speak in a strange, abstracted way.

"I see an island in the north and on it a great tree. You and the tree are one. You, like the tree, will provide food, shelter, and courage for the people."

She closed her eyes. The short audience was over.

Aurelia pulled him to the opposite side, where a man was seated. He had thick, curly hair and wore a short sky blue tunic and intricately worked leather boots that rested on another beautiful carpet. In one hand, he held a large hammer, and in the other a golden dish. A very large, washed and manicured dog sat panting at his side.

"Put a coin in the dish!" Aurelia whispered.

Lucius added a coin to the others in the golden platter. But this time, the man spoke only to Aurelia:

"You will travel far … and be fortunate in love." He closed his eyes.

A young man and woman stepped out of the shadows and guided Lucius and Aurelia to the flap that served as an exit, from which they were ushered out into the blinding sunlight of the late afternoon.

"What happens now?" Lucius asked.

He would not have been surprised if she had said they would fly or stand on their heads for a week.

"There is more to come, but do you remember what the Goddess said to you?"

"Goddess? You mean that woman who was seated on the large chair?"

"No, silly, that woman was the vessel. It was the blessed Nantos-uelta who spoke through the woman, just as Sucellos spoke through the man."

"Who are Nantosuelta and Sucellos?" Lucius asked.

"Nantosuelta is the raven goddess. Her other name is Winding River. She appears as a dove when she is in her mother form. At those times, she blesses your hearth and home. She appears as a raven when she is in her war goddess form. The water you saw at the foot of the throne is from a spring from which a great river is born near one of her temples. It symbolizes her ability to heal and to prophesy. She can see between the worlds.

"The God who spoke to me through the curly haired man is her consort. He is the sky god, Sucellos, who is also called the Good Striker because his voice can be heard in the thunder, and because he sends his lightning as a blessing to fertilize the Earth Mother. He too is a great healer and a prophet. He said I would be lucky in love!"

Aurelia smiled as she reached up to touch Lucius's face. This time, he held her gaze, but his face went the color of a freshly cut fig.

5

"A re you hungry?" Aurelia asked, after hearing a long, low grumble emanate from the general direction of Lucius's stomach.

"I'm ready to eat anything! I have plenty of coins; shall I buy us some of those horn-shaped cakes?"

The scent of cinnamon rose from cakes freshly baked on a fire. It was driving him to distraction, and he realized he had not eaten any-thing since the day before.

"You don't have to buy food at the festival. Those are special cakes meant as offerings to the gods. I have many friends and relations here; we can easily find a meal! Follow me."

She led him through a confusing neighborhood of goatskin and linen tarps, and he wondered how she could possibly know where she was going. Then they finally reached the far edge of the encampment on the side opposite to the beach.

"See the throng of people high on that hill? They are sharing a meal with the dead. We can join them," she said gaily.

Once again, his breath choked in his throat. "Eat with the dead? Surely not!"

"Oh, yes," she replied. "We do it every year at this time."

Lucius was used to mournful funeral processions and burials on Inissi Leuca, garnished with plenty of doleful preaching about the Day of Judgment and the horrors of hell. The idea of happy communion with dead people was something uniquely bizarre.

They followed a well-worn path up the grassy slope and soon came upon a group of Aurelia's relations amidst the other picnicking families. Her father, Melor, Uncle Sadwrn, Aunt Aude, her ten-year-old sister Breaca, her mother, Weluela, and her ancient grandparents Anna and Cadfan sat dressed in wide yellow straw hats and pale tunics to protect them from the blazing sun. They waved joyfully in Aurelia's direction the moment they recognized her. The family was comfortably ensconced on woolen blankets spread in front of an ancient stone chair. They were all lean, tanned, and muscular, with broad, toothy grins.

"Ho! I see you have caught yourself a nice fish for after the fires!" said Aunt Aude with a smile and a twinkle in her eyes.

"More like a whale by the size of him!" added her mother with a wink. Everyone laughed.

Embarrassed by their joking, Lucius had no idea what "after the fires" meant, but he instinctively hunched his shoulders to shrink himself down to more closely match the family's stature.

"This is my new friend Lucius, from Inissi Leuca," Aurelia declared proudly.

A slight silence and a meeting of glances came at the mention of the *Cristaidi* isle.

"I have never … actually met anyone from that island," said her grandfather, picking his words with care. He had heard of terrible events further inland; some monks were known to be violent. But it was Giamonios, after all, and peace and hospitality were due by custom to everyone who set foot within the festival grounds.

The family invited Lucius and Aurelia to sit and passed them wooden plates and cups, green beans pickled with whole garlic cloves, red, green, and black olives dripping in oil, a large round loaf of barley bread, and the remnants of a huge wheel of goat cheese that had held the place of honor on a platter in the middle of the blankets. A basketful of dried apples, dates, and raisins and a dish of fresh strawberries followed.

They also passed around a goatskin of *uinom*, and every so often one of the family rose to squeeze some of the crimson liquid into a little silver cup placed on the stone seat. Samples of every food filled a plate on the grass before the chair.

Only after Lucius had cleaned two bowlfuls of food and carefully mopped up every last drop of oil with a piece of barley bread did he find his tongue. "Why is that rock carved to look like a chair? And why is that cup sitting there?"

Grandmother Anna replied, squirting a bit more *uinom* into the silver cup. "This is the Hill of the Ancestors. Our family, going back for thousands of sun cycles, is buried here; we're sitting on their bones that lie under the grass. The chair is for them, so they can sit here and watch over the countryside. From that chair, you can see the peninsula, our farm, the beach, the gathering, everything!" She waved her arm to emphasize the glorious extent of the view.

"We're sitting on their graves?" Lucius felt slightly sick, as if he were falling backwards into a tilting world. He had been taught that it was disrespectful to even walk over a grave, though he knew that the monks and brothers sometimes dug a bit of earth from the grave of a holy person or a martyr for use in their healing work.

"Oh, yes, we come here every year at festival time to keep our ancestors company and to give them food. Our children and grandchildren will do it for us one day too," said Aurelia happily. "Don't the *Cristaidi* feed their dead?"

"Er … no, not like that," said Lucius. "We might lay flowers on a grave or speak to our dead, and we pray for them all the time. But we are not supposed to desecrate a grave by actually sitting on it."

"That's silly," said Breaca with an all-knowing air as she added another strawberry to the dish before the stone seat.

6

Martinus and Isidore heard a mysterious thumping sound outside the walls of the guesthouse that continued at intervals throughout the night. Added to it was the distant thunder of drums from the other side of the bay. It had not been a good night for sleeping.

Rising well before Lauds, they followed the thumping sound, which led them through damp grasses to a tiny, round, wattle-and-daub cell with a conical roof of willow twigs, built at a distance from all the other buildings. Just as they approached the structure, a fist punched through the wall, startling them both. A stream of oaths followed. Clearly, whoever had punched through the wall was in pain.

"Can we help you, brother?" Martinus inquired, peering through the opening.

There was a long exhale, then a plaintively miserable voice. "No one can help me. I still have five more days."

"Of solitude, you mean? What terrible sin has caused you to be set apart in this way?" Martinus asked.

"I left the island in a curach!"

"Why did you leave the confines of the island, brother?"

"I had to get away. This island is too small for me!"

Martinus spoke in a low whisper so that the confined brother would not overhear.

"His actions show a certain…hmm…*initiative*, don't you think, Isidore? Perhaps this brother is best suited to be one of our recruits. He has a strong arm to gouge through a mud and wicker wall like that!"

Abbott Mihael was horrified to see Martinus, Isidore, and Teilo arrive together for Prime. When the other monks and brothers left the chapel to begin their morning chores, he followed the three out into the early morning fog.

"What is going on here? I haven't given permission for this miscreant to leave his cell!"

"He is no longer guilty. I set him free," said Martinus mildly. "I intend to make him one of my own. We will ferry to the mainland tonight and put an end to that wretched mayhem over there."

Abbott Mihael was speechless at Martinus's presumption, but there was nothing further that he could say or do. He could only hope that Teilo would hold his tongue and say nothing about the other two boys. He watched as the three walked together into the Great House, where Teilo stuffed himself liberally at the breakfast table, eating three times the usual portion of goat cheese and bread.

7

The sun is setting, so we'd better start down to prepare for the ritual," said Weluela, already packing the leftovers into a large, round wicker basket.

The family stood to shake out crumbs and fold blankets. They poured the *uinom* from the little silver cup lovingly onto the ground and carefully overturned the contents of the plate of food onto the grass in front of the chair.

"The spirits have had their feast, and we can go," said Grandmother Anna, and the family started the hike back down from the grassy hill.

Once the sun fell below the line of the sand dunes, a mist and a chill began to settle on the camp.

"I forgot to bring a cloak," Lucius confided to Aurelia when they were back at the tent. The rest of the family retied their hair and brushed and smoothed their clothes inside in preparation for the evening festivities. Everyone had a wreath of herbs and flowers for his or her hair, with long colorful ribbons hanging behind.

"Don't worry about the cold," said Aurelia with a mysterious smile. "We will be moving most of the night; anyway, there will be fires everywhere. This is the time to let go and trust in the spirits. Let the God and Goddess of the festival protect you and guide you. It's the best way to experience our ceremony."

Lucius thought briefly about the monks and brothers on Inissi Leuca, who would be at Vespers this very moment, and how strange they would feel to be where he was now. He thought Teilo would probably enjoy the novelty, but Justan would worry himself to a frazzle working out exactly how venial or mortal a sin he was committing. He offered up a silent prayer for himself, his friends, and for everyone at the festival:

> *Exaudi nos, Domine sancte, Pater omnipotens, aeterne Deus,*
> *et mittere digneris sanctum Angelum tuum de coelis, qui custodiat,*
> *foveat, protegat, visitet atque defendat omnes habitantes in hoc*
> *habitaculo.*

Aurelia did not hear the words, but she caught his expression. "You are so serious!" she said, giving him a playful tickle in the ribs.

"You two run ahead and enjoy the evening!" said Weluela with a smile.

Lucius and Aurelia parted the tent flaps, leaving the others to their dressing. Lucius snuck furtive glances at Aurelia, noticing how the garland of roses in her hair set off the smoothness of her skin. Aunt Aude had produced a wreath of bay laurel for him, which he wore gladly, thinking it helped him fit in with the other celebrants. In the darkness, Lucius saw tiny twinkling lights dotting the hill where they had shared their afternoon meal with the family.

"What are all those lights?" he asked, moved by the spectacle.

"Those are candles and oil lamps set out to honor the dead. They too must have a little fire to cheer them on this night."

They made their way to the center of the gathering, where a large crowd waited; for what, Lucius had no idea. Many of them carried lit torches, but others held massive tree branches topped by balls of linen soaked in oil and wax.

The beat of drums began softly at first and gradually built to a loud, steady rhythm. Flutes, cymbals, and voices started a hymn and, after what felt like an eternity, a group of dancers appeared, waving large branches of willow and other greenery. The singing picked up tempo and volume as a second group of dancers followed the first, wafting incense towards the crowd with black and white birds' wings.

A couple appeared that Lucius recognized as the Goddess and God from earlier that day. They were dressed in flowing scarlet robes and had elaborate wreaths of flowers and ribbons on their heads. They moved in same abstracted way that they had earlier, as if only half in the waking world. Behind them was yet another group of dancers; these beckoned to the crowd to follow and kept the beat with cymbals tied to their fingers and bells on their feet. The large crowd slowly fell in behind.

The huge procession coiled out of the tent city towards a long avenue of stones. At intervals between the stone rows, men held torches aloft so that no one would fall. The drumming and singing grew even louder as excitement built in the crowd. Aurelia held tight to Lucius's arm.

When the line of celebrants had reached the end of the stone rows the crowd parted, some going left, some going to the right, to fill a large circular enclosure at the end of the processional route. The dancers filled the center of the circle, rhythmically waving their branches high and then sweeping them low to the ground.

The God and the Goddess moved into the very center of the ring and began a slow, erotic dance as the other dancers circled the center of the ritual space. The drums picked up their pace and the singing grew louder again as the God slowly parted the robes of the Goddess and caressed her bare breasts so that everyone could see. The Goddess arched backwards as he kissed her breasts and her body, now bared fully to the crowd.

The drums pounded frantically, and the dancers whirled and leaped. The God entered the Goddess as they sank to the ground in a heaving, pulsing mound. As though sparks had flared from their bodies, couples took their cue and paired off into the surrounding bushes. Those who held unlit torches touched them to the torches already aflame and sped off into the darkness.

Aurelia's grip on Lucius tightened. She looked up at him expectantly, her face flushed.

"You don't … ?" he asked, blushing furiously and knowing that she did.

"Don't be afraid. This is a festival of love. Every couple that joins in this ritual blesses the earth and strengthens the growing grain. Others across the land are in the fields now, making love in the furrows of their farms, under the full moon. The energy of our ritual fires is being carried by the torch bearers to villages in the distant hills. It is a time of magic! Can't you feel it?"

Aurelia stroked his chest, felt his nipples under his tunic, and pressed her lower body against his. He did feel the magic; pungent warmth spread rapidly through him as he grew stiff with a hunger he had never known. He wanted her.

He took her hand, guiding her towards a dark patch of trees. Aurelia folded her arms about his middle and one hand circled the mound of his buttock, caressing it as they walked. Lucius was drunk with feeling; nothing else existed.

"Dominus vobiscum."

The words were a cold bucket of sea water over his body. "What?" Lucius exclaimed, startled out of his dream.

"I said *Dominus vobiscum*. Surely you remember the response?"

Lucius wheeled around to find Martinus, Isidore, and Teilo standing there. Isidore moved quickly to push Aurelia roughly aside.

"No! Don't do that!" Lucius yelled.

Aurelia cried out in shock and fear as Isidore moved her even farther away.

"These are good and loving people, you can't treat them this way!" Lucius cried.

"Idiot!" growled Martinus, his hand reaching to grab Lucius by the hair. "You are in mortal danger and so is everyone else in this disgusting place! Teilo and Isidore, tie his hands, and we'll take him back to the ferry. Drag him if you have to. He will be saved!"

34

Lucius's hands were tied behind his back with Teilo's belt and, since he wouldn't stop yelling, Isidore stuffed his leather money pouch into his mouth.

"Sorry, Lucius, it's for your own good!" said Teilo, already a dedicated convert to Martinus's ways.

As they dragged him towards the beach, Lucius saw the results of their zeal. While everyone else had been attending the ritual, the three had ripped ribbons down from trees, overturned altars, smashed statues of gods and goddesses, and generally created as much mayhem as they could to disrupt the proceedings. They had set fire to the red tent and all of its contents, including the live birds in their wicker cages.

"No one will sing to the Pagan gods, drink to the Pagan gods, eat with the Pagan gods, or light candles to the Pagan gods! Not if I have anything to say about it!" Martinus fumed. "This whoring and debauchery will stop!"

They paid the waiting ferryman—who looked none too happy at serving them—boarded, and shoved Lucius down to make him sit. Lucius saw that the ferryman was trembling in fear, calling on Sucellos to save him. Martinus stalked over to the ferryman and slapped him hard on the face.

"You will be silent, man, or I will curse you to hell!"

The ferryman closed his mouth tight and bent to his work.

Martinus turned towards shore and lifted his hands. Fingers splayed wide, palms facing the mainland, he cried, "I order you *daemones*, by the powers of the God of Hosts, to leave this place! I command you in the name of Raphael, Israel, Ragouel, and Agathoel to leave! I cast a ring of protection around these people, around this place! Out, *daemones*, out!"

Teilo and Isidore were hugely impressed by Martinus's evident magical powers. Lucius was horrified, his heart breaking at the thought of how hurt Aurelia and her family would be. Worst of all, they would think he had brought this upon them. Then he began to weep.

8

Martinus rang the bell that called the monks and brothers to the Great House. He ordered Isidore and Teilo to remove Lucius to a solitary cell and to bar the door with a stout oaken log. Justan had been let out of his wicker cell the day before on the orders of Abbott Mihael. The mild piety of the boy made the abbott feel lenient.

When the rest of the community was present and seated at the long table used for meals and almost all other work, Martinus clambered onto the high seat usually reserved for the abbott.

"If thy brother, son, daughter, or wife entice thee, secretly saying, 'Let us go and serve other gods' ... thou shalt surely kill them. That is what Deuteronomy tells us, unless you have forgotten," said Martinus. "I have been very lenient in this matter. Our wayward brother is safe in his cell, doing penance for his terrible transgressions, and I have hurt no one.

"Let this episode be a lesson to the *Pagani* on shore. I will soon be made bishop, and I will allow no more of these repulsive gatherings. I am quite sure that the *Pagani* understand the message I, Isidore, and Brother Teilo have given. I expect all of you to follow my example and work to stamp out any further heresy.

"Anyone performing animal sacrifice will be forced from their home and excommunicated. If you find a Pagan temple, you will pull it down, rebuild it, and reconsecrate it for our use. Everyone must attend a Christian church or have their property seized and be sent into exile. Any lawyer, teacher, bureaucrat, or noble who professes to be a Pagan will be publicly mocked, disgraced, and driven from office. Pagan fountains and wells are to be rededicated to Christian saints or else filled in, and their so-called sacred trees and groves will be cut down. Do you understand me?"

Abbott Mihael stood to speak. "The banning of sacrifices will be a great hardship for the poor. Many of them have no meat, save that which is provided at funeral feasts and festival gatherings."

"Tell the rich to offer public meals on Christian feast days and holidays! What difference does it make? They only offer food to the poor to curry political favor with their neighbors and to gain status in their eyes. One day is as good as another for political gain.

"You must ban all processions unless they end at the grave of a martyr or a saint. Tell them it is a useless waste to light candles for the dead. Candles are only to be used to light the darkness of a home or to honor a Christian shrine."

Having received his orders from Martinus, Abbott Mihael sighed in frustration. "To think that all I ever really wanted was a simple hermit's life by the sea," he muttered under his breath, quietly enough that no one would hear.

9

That night, Teilo crept out of the dormitory to sneak a visit with Lucius, impounded in the same tiny wattle-and-daub cell that Teilo had occupied before.

"Brother!" he whispered through the hole his own fist had made. "I have brought you bread and cheese from supper." He extended a loaf of bread through the opening, followed by several hunks of cheese. Lucius grabbed them eagerly.

"Why did you do it?" Lucius asked. "The people on the mainland will be devastated by your destruction of everything that is most sacred to them."

"We had to. It was for the good of their souls, and your soul too!"

"I have been thinking," said Lucius. "Mihael instructs us that serenity, gentleness, and patience are the qualities we should aspire to when dealing with others. He always tells us to avoid anger, arrogance, and discourtesy. This destruction is not what we have learned here. I don't understand. Whatever happened to compassion and charity—to divine love?"

"The world is changing, Lucius. Martinus represents the new way, and I am proud to be a part of it. He is a powerful man; he has even come to the attention of the church in Rome! The more important he becomes, the more important I will be too."

"Those are not the words of the Brother Teilo I stole apples with. What you did to the *Pagani* and this kind of talk makes me very sad."

"I want more than stolen apples. I'm leaving Inissi Leuca behind. I'm a grown man now; I can make my own decisions, and I want to see the world!"

Teilo walked into the night and did not return to the little cell.

Lucius thought endlessly about the fate of Aurelia and her kin. What he had seen of the *Pagani* showed him that they were simple and honest. They fed each other and their ancestors, honored their gods, and did magic to help the earth. They were not evil people, as he had been led to believe. The only evil he had witnessed was the destruction wrought by Martinus. If this was true Christianity—for Martinus was favored by Rome—he wanted no part of it.

Alongside his fear for Aurelia and her relations lay his ever-present wish to find his own blood family, no matter the cost. A few nights later, he smashed an empty chamber pot and cut a hole in the wall with a large shard. In the grey light of pre-dawn, he collected his clothing, water-skin, and blanket, and slipped through the wicker and mud wall. He crawled over the massive *vallum* that sheltered the monastery from the sea winds, walked the shoreline until he found the little leather boat that Teilo and Justan had left hidden in the usual clump of bushes, and paddled across to the mainland.

10

An ancient hawthorn dipped its roots into the stream that coursed through the woodland clearing where Ethne, Ruadh, and the other Druid had carved out a life in the wilderness. Because the *Cristaidi* now had firm control of the Ard-Ri, the *flaith*, and the warriors of the island, the Druid were pushed away from the centers of power they had held since ancient times.

The Cauldron of Sea, a large bronze vessel that the Druid brought with them when they left In Medon, nestled between exposed roots on the opposite side of the tree. The roots had grown so tightly around the cauldron in recent years that it now seemed an organic outgrowth of the trunk. It was hard to keep the water free of falling leaves, berries, and blossoms, but the vessel was so close to the stream that scooping out and refilling the water daily was less of a chore than it had been in the old *nemed* of the Ard-Ri's *rath*. In those days, the neophytes had to make a daily trek to the river with leather buckets.

The hawthorn tree and the sacred cauldron were the focal points of ritual for the small settlement. The Cauldron of Sea was used for scrying and as a sacred well to hold silver jewelry and coin offerings from those who visited the sanctuary. These and other sacrifices were carefully buried in votive pits scattered around the property as gifts for the gods, the land spirits, and the ancestors.

A stone-lined fire pit stood to one side of the tree and served as the fire altar, but the Druid no longer maintained a perpetual fire within its confines; wood was too precious, and the effort was needed for more immediate survival. Instead, they lit a bonfire of nine sacred woods or one made entirely of oak and kept it burning for three days and nights on each of the fire festivals.

They prayed before the ritual fire day and night while it was lit and gave it offerings of butter, oil, and dried herbs. They also fed Waters of Life to the flames, the sacred liquid that healed the sick and calmed the mind. While pouring the golden draught upon the flames, they visualized the amber nectar rising to the sky realm of the gods—a fitting gift.

The fire, like the Cauldron of Sea, was used for scrying and divination just as before, when the Druid had kept their perpetual fire in the *nemed* of the Ard-Ri. Folk from the outlying villages still came with their questions, and the Druid would read the answers in the faces and singing voices of the embers.

Afterward, the Druid carefully sifted the ashes of the ritual fire and preserved them to be used in the making of *siabainn*, adding extra magical healing power. Cakes of *siabainn* made with sacred ash were distributed to the sick or troubled in spirit. All these things were done as they had been done from ancient times, but there was no denying that now these performances were crimped and spare. The rituals in the little clearing were but a pale shadow of the magnificent ceremonies the Druid had once supervised before they lost status in the religious and social life of the tribes.

"What cannot be helped must be put up with," said Ethne philosophically, eyeing the tiny ritual space with a thought to the upcoming Beltaine rites. "I remember when we led a hundred of the Ard-Ri's cattle between the fires, to bless them on their way to the summer pastures," she mused, a little sadly.

Ruadh enfolded her within his arms to shield her from such thoughts, planting a gentle kiss on her forehead.

Ethne was Ard-Ban-Drui of the little tribe of Forest Druids. In her youth, she had served for many years in the Forest House, tending to the sick and wounded who came under her care, until she fell in love with Ruadh, a wounded *fennidi* who had been brought to her for healing. Eventually, she was called by the Ard-Drui to serve Crimthann, the Ard-Ri of the time, and to marry him. When Crimthann was killed in battle, Ethne rejoined Ruadh, her handfast partner.

Ruadh had once been a battle leader of the *fennidi* and, as Ethne's life mate, now supervised the security of the Forest School, patrolling the surrounding woodlands and roads and teaching the younger Druid the arts of archery and swordplay. By now he was a Drui himself in all but title, having had full access to the rituals and classes offered at the school.

They found contentment in each other despite the circumscribed life they led, but there was a deeper shadow between them. Their infant son, Ruadhán, had disappeared without a trace with his nursemaid, many years before. They never had another child.

Some nights Ethne still woke with a start, thinking she heard Ruadhán crying. She would pace the darkness alone, a physical part of her stuck in the Otherworld, waiting to be reclaimed. That pain was part of who she was now. Often Ruadh would find her and try to give her comfort, but his own loss was just as deep. Too many times, his gentle kisses led to nothing more than a weary embrace. The disappearance of their son cast their passion with guilt, and the ever-present work of the school took what remained of their energy.

During the daylight, however, Ethne had Daire, the princeling born to her earlier marriage to the Ard-Ri Crimthann, whom she and Ruadh had adopted as their own. He was a strapping youth of almost twenty summers who excelled in his studies and had become Ruadh's right hand in hunting and battle.

They also had Aífe of the golden curls and the strange emerald eyes that sparkled like dew on the summer grass. She had come to the old *nemed* of the Ard-Ri as an infant, the child of Druid parents who had died in a fire. Aífe was an expert healer and the one most often at Ethne's side when the wounded and sick came for succor. She was brilliant in her studies and driven to excel in every subject of Druidic practice and lore.

"Aífe has a real gift and should be taught the deepest secrets of the Druid, just as I was in my youth. There is so much more she should know," said Ethne with a deep sigh.

"We are doing what we can to keep most of the old ways secure. Passing them on to future generations is our best hope," replied Ruadh.

"Maybe even for ourselves in our next incarnation," Ethne added. She was determined that this was not to be the end of the Druid story and would do anything to protect and ensure their traditions.

By and large, Ethne and Ruadh were satisfied, knowing that similar Druidic colleges were thriving here and there, hidden away in forests all over the island. The Druid school they had created was a haven of peace and scholarship, and those in need of healing still came to the Forest House in the clearing, as they had for generations.

The land was happy too. The fruit trees and blackberries at the edges of the fields were flourishing, and wooden beehives hummed on their benches beneath the apple trees. Fields had been cleared for barley, oats, and rye, and there was a well-established garden of healing worts and vegetables that kept them well supplied.

Over the years, grateful visitors had donated pigs, goats, chickens, and even a cow. The members of the school had built a willow-thatched timber barn surrounded by its own palisade, where the goats and pigs kept each other company and chickens roosted and laid their eggs on shelves high in the rafters.

The cow, which was regarded as a near-human member of the community, had her own private pen and willow-thatched stable filled with clean straw and surrounded by a low fence over which she could view the daily activities of the settlement. She was called Gnóe for her shiny white hide, limpid brown eyes, and pink nose.

The men had erected a wooden smokehouse to cure meats, another for the drying of grains, and several new round houses with conical roofs of willow-thatch to house students and visitors. Ethne and Ruadh shared the old hut that Ethne had once occupied alone, and the stone *tech ind allais* still stood near the stream, ready to receive those in need of a sweat cure to purify their blood and warm their bones.

Clothru and Damán, former apprentices from the old *nemed* of the Ard-Ri, were now handfasted and the proud parents of Cathail, Cuill, and Gaine Óg. All afternoon, they had managed to keep the children seated quietly under an enormous oak tree by bribing each with a promised section of honeycomb if they could concentrate the rest of the day on their studies.

"By the end of the today, I want you to know all your trees," said Damán. "Now, who can tell me the poetic meanings of birch?"

All three raised their hands eagerly, but Cathail, the oldest, spoke aloud. "Faded trunk and fair hair, most silvery of skin!"

"Right," said Damán. "Who can tell me about hazel?"

This time, all three answered in chorus. "Fairest of trees, friend of cracking!"

"Wish we had some now," Cuill muttered. They had not eaten since the sun was high, and his stomach was growling.

"All right, now who can tell me about oak? Gaine Óg, can you recite the words?" Gaine Óg had thoroughly memorized her trees, but at age four had a limited grasp of the meanings.

"Highest of bushes, a carpenter's work," she offered by rote.

And so it continued as one by one the children made their recitations:

Ash: "checking of peace" because it is used to make spears and bows;

Rowan: "delight of eye" for its beautiful white blossoms and red berries;

Hawthorn: "blanching of face" because the poets use it to satirize their foes by sticking its thorns into clay poppets;

Alder: "shield of warrior bands" because it is used to make warrior's shields and because it bleeds red when cut;

Apple: "shelter of a hind" because the deer love to eat them and shelter under them in winter;

Vine: "condition of slaughter" because *fion* is red as blood and fit to be offered as a sacrifice;

Willow: "sacred to poets" because from its wood, harps are made;

Blackthorn: "strongest of red" because it is used to make a red dye, and because it is used to make shillelaghs, which cause terrible red wounds;

Holly: "fires of coal" used to make charcoal;

Ivy: "sweeter than grasses" because the cows and bees like to eat it in the cold season when there is nothing else;

Furze: "wounder of horses" because it grows on rough soil and tears at the horse's legs;

Elder: "intensest of blushes" because its blossoms are used for fevers that cause a red face and because of its red twigs, berries, and juice; it is sacred to mothers and a great healer of children, never to be burned;

Heather: "in cold dwellings" because it grows in cold, damp places and helps the cough;

Reed: "robe of physicians" because it is used to blow powdered medicines into a sick person's throat and onto a wound;

Silver Fir: "beginnings of an answer" because it is the tallest tree in the forest and symbolizes the far-seeing of the visionary;

White Poplar: "synonym for a friend" because it is used to make shields (and who is your best shield but a true friend?); and

Yew: "oldest of woods" that is planted in graveyards and is said to live forever.

"Now you know the poetic meaning of the trees," said Damán, satisfied with their work. "Each tree is also a letter of the alphabet, a musical note, and a finger position in sign language. These triple meanings make up part of the secret language of the Forest Druids. You will be able to speak to other Druids using these kennings, and no one will be the wiser. But that is for another day."

Clothru added, "Tomorrow, we will build two fires with nine sacred woods. We will drive Gnóe between those fires to bless and purify her for summer. The fires must be so close together that her white hide is singed brown. Then we will have our own little Beltaine feast!"

Clothru and Damán gazed at each other over the children's heads, recalling the magnificent fires of their own childhoods and the runners who once came from every province to dip their torches into the sacred flames. Their world had changed so much.

11

Áife was determined to make this Beltaine a happy one for the Forest Druids. She felt the disappointment of the older members as they tried to put out of their minds all the grandeur of the past and saw how they struggled to make the best of things as they were.

With the all-important fire festival at the start of summer, the feast of Beltaine, about to begin, she thought deeply about the symbolism of the day and how to express it in ceremony. She had secreted away snowy white eggshells for weeks, blowing out the yolk and whites through carefully bored holes at either end. She saved all the insides and added them to endless caudles and omelets. She had accumulated a wicker basket full of the fragile shells, which she dyed by soaking them first in apple cider vinegar and water and then in a hot brew of green carrot tops. The result was a sunny yellow that reminded her of Beltaine morning.

Golden marsh marigolds were in full bloom in and around the stream, heralding summer as they always did, and the holly bushes were just putting forth their tiny white blossoms. She wandered the grounds for days and finally settled on one particularly gorgeous holly bush standing on a little hill, facing east. On Beltaine Eve, as the others prepared the fires, she secretly decorated the bush with fresh yellow marsh marigold blossoms and hung it with the yellow shells. It was now a *bíle samrata*.

On Beltaine morn, everyone woke before dawn and bathed in the morning dew—a magical aid to beauty—then walked to the ritual site to wait for the sun to rise high enough to strike the water in the Cauldron of the Sea. When the first rays of sunlight rippled across the waters, everyone thrust in a hand to capture the sun in the water; it was especially lucky to be the first to hold the sun-blessed liquid.

"When fire and water mix, that is when the power of magic is strongest," said Ethne. "The world is made of fire and water, male and female, summer and winter, dark and light. From these polarities, all things arise. This is why we drive cows between the fires on this day. Cows are creatures of the moon and give us milk, a type of sacred water, which feeds and sustains us.

"Passing the cows between the fires keeps the world in balance. It is the same reason that we drive horses, creatures of the sun, through water at Lugnasad to purify them."

"I have a surprise for you all!" said Aífe. Her smile was much like the newly risen sun. "Follow me."

She led them to the little *bíle samrata*, standing in splendor in the rays of the rising sun. The children gasped.

"She has the soul of a poet!" declared Ruadh, proudly.

The little company of Druid clasped hands and began an impromptu circling dance to honor the sweet and lovely tree.

"The fairies and the spirits of this place are very happy with what you have done, Aífe," said Ethne. "They love beauty and dancing and laughter. You have given us a new way to honor the start of summer, and I thank you for it."

Ethne was moved by the *bíle samrata* and happy that Aífe had shown them this gentle direction for private Druid rites in the forest. She knew that this was the world in which they now lived.

That night, as she rested in Ruadh's arms, Ethne conceived a plan. "Aífe would have been chosen to be a *ban-fili* in the old days. Her *imbas* is strong, and with a little training, she could almost certainly be a vessel, a voice for the High Ones. We have given her all we can in this place. There is only one other who could work with her to develop her gifts; I think we need to take her to Gaine."

Gaine was the ancient Ard-Ban-Drui of the *nemed* that was once the focus for Druid ritual activity in the island. When Ethne, Ruadh, and the others left in the wake of the missionaries' repressions and violent incursions, Gaine had chosen to stay behind, taking spiritual responsibility for the care of the villagers and Druid who would not, or could not, leave the *tuath* of In Medon.

"Gaine must be very frail by now, if she is even still alive," said Ruadh.

"We would have known if she had traveled to the Otherworld," replied Ethne quietly. "Anyway, it is long past time to see to Aífe's welfare. Aífe can tend to Gaine if she is sickly. Aífe would learn much at Gaine's side."

A few days after Beltaine, Ethne, Ruadh, and Aífe packed their traveling food, cloaks, and packs. As always, Ruadh wore his intricately worked red leather scabbard and sword, strapped to his leg and hidden under his cloak, and Ethne and Aífe were well supplied with dirks and knives hidden in their clothing. Ethne and Ruadh left their large golden torcs, symbols of their true rank, in a cedar box in the Forest House, choosing instead to wear golden triskellean on leather thongs about their necks, because these could be easily hidden under woolen tunics.

They set off, leaving Daire, Clothru, and Damán in charge of the Forest School. All three were dressed in muted greys, browns, and greens to more easily blend into the forest if danger threatened, and as they walked, Ruadh and Ethne marveled at the changes they witnessed. Everywhere they went, trees had been felled and large tracts of rye and other grains had sprung up.

"The *Cristaidi* tell the people to cut down the trees to stop our ancient reverence for the tree spirits," Ethne explained to Aífe as they walked. "The first trees they cut were the yews, because they are sacred to us for their ancient spirits, their medicine, and their healing powers."

Ethne's heart seared with pain, and a lump grew in her throat as she spoke. She would forever remember the day the *Cristaidi* came to cut down the stately yews. Many had stood and wept that terrible day, bowing their heads in shame and crying bitter tears in disbelief.

For her, and for all the Druid, the ancient yews were tree people. Some even took them for gods. To the Druid, all trees were revered as venerable and noble spirits who had given their wood, their lives, and their medicine forever, for the health and survival of the tribes. When the *Cristaidi* finished killing the trees, the *Pagani* stole back in the night and left offerings of butter, cheese, honey, sweet herbs, and apple cider to recompense the earth and the tree spirits for their loss. But it was a poor exchange.

"Next, they told the people to cut down the hazels, even though the tribes have depended on them since time began for their sweet nuts and their healing bark. They know these trees are sacred to us because they haveheard the stories of the magical Well of Segais and of the nine hazels that stand over it, and of the salmon of wisdom who rise to eat the nuts as they fall," said Ruadh.

"What they don't understand is that the Well of Wisdom is a Druidic mystery," Ethne added. "It lives in the Otherworld, and even if all the hazels in the world were cut down, it would still flourish. The salmon who eat the nuts as they fall are the Druid. Each time a Drui learns a bit of our inner teachings, they gain a spot, a mark of their learning. The hazelnut symbolizes the compact wisdom of the Drui, the knowledge that she or he carries in their head, hidden beyond reach."

"Is that why you always carry hazelnuts and acorns in your pockets?" asked Aífe.

"Yes, they remind us to always use our wisdom," Ethne replied.

"But what is the meaning of the well? In some stories, it is at the bottom of the ocean; in other stories, it is described as the source of a great river."

"The well is the eternal, inexhaustible source of wisdom that is within everyone, if you just know how to find it," replied Ethne. "The secret path to the Source is the perfection of the five senses. This is why we Druid are disciplined in our lives and ways, and why we develop our listening, our speech, our seeing, and all of our senses. The ultimate perfection of the five streams of knowledge results in what we call *Ecnae Bratánech*, or salmon wisdom. It is when we gain the ability to answer our own questions," said Ethne, reminding Aífe of her lessons from childhood.

"The salmon is born in an inland stream and unfailingly finds its way to the ocean. It spends many sun cycles in deep waters, miles from shore, and then returns unerringly to the exact stream of its birth. In this same way, you can go deep into meditation and find your own answers to any question by following the stream of the silence within. It will take you all the way back to the Source of All if you but ask."

"Oh," was all Aífe said, but she practiced silence for the rest of the afternoon, soundlessly repeating all she had heard and committing it to memory, as she had been trained to do from infancy.

When they reached the Cave of the Bears, Ruadh and Aífe went into the surrounding woods to cut soft pine boughs for bedding while Ethne stood at the mouth of the cave and stared into its depths. She had created so much of her life here and left so much of it behind as well. She had not known when they set out that day what parts of herself she might find in this deep and quiet place. In the first days of their love, she and Ruadh had given themselves to each other here. It had been a safe hollow where their hearts could meet and rest. It may have been the beginning place for the little lost life that she mourned.

Ethne closed her eyes and said a prayer. She knew her heart would never heal from this grief, but she asked for solace in those she loved and in the days that were given to them. She pulled a small phial from her pouch and sprinkled the Waters of Life before the cave's entrance and took out beeswax candles to be set into the recesses of the rock walls. Thus purified, she entered the cave with gratitude.

When Ruadh and Aífe returned, they laid the pine boughs in mounds on the cave floor and spread their blankets over them, three soft beds for three weary bodies. Ethne unpacked the cooking vessels, the strips of meat, the loaf of bread, and the dried grains.

"Aífe," she asked, "would you please go down to the stream and fill this pot with water? I'll gather up dry branches and twigs so that we can make a large fire for the evening."

Aífe went willingly and Ethne stood to follow, but Ruadh came up behind her and encircled her in his arms. He brushed her hair aside and put his lips to her neck. "Our love lives in this place, Ethne. Do you feel it?"

She let herself sink into his hold, let herself slide into that place that was only theirs. It had been so long—so long since there was nothing but Ruadh and her, so long since there had been anything but work and sadness. "Yes," she whispered. "I feel this cave holds our first togetherness and our first hopes." Tears came and she turned, raising her face to his. His mouth covered hers, and he pushed her gently into the darkness against the wall of the cave. He touched all the curves and arcs of her face. He traced the outline of her mouth, then bent again and kissed her hard. He cupped her breasts and felt her nipples, already swollen under her woolen tunic. He lifted her against the wall and she raised one leg, curled it tightly around his back, and welcomed him with her soul and her body. She took in the joy she thought she had lost forever, and he cried out once as if in answer to her deepest question.

12

Lucius paddled furiously to avoid being spotted by the monks and brothers when they rose for Prime. Putting aside thoughts of finding his own kin, now he thought of nothing but Aurelia and her family. He felt personally responsible for the disaster at the Giamonios festival.

Where had she said they lived? He would walk the peninsula until he found them, no matter how long, at whatever cost. What he would do once he found them, he didn't know, but he had to see that they were safe.

He paddled the little leather craft as close to shore as he was able, then climbed out and pulled it onto the shingle. He found a cluster of scrub and hid the boat and paddles deep inside, covered with leafy branches and seaweed, and climbed a sandy hill in hopes of a better view and more solid footing closer inland. Nearing the crest of a large dune, he dropped to a crawl so as not to be seen and peered over the other side, disbelieving.

Romani covered the area. An entire centuria swarmed over the landscape; worse, local Galli sat in desolate clusters on the ground, hands on their heads, soldiers standing over them with swords drawn. Bronze helmets and bronze-trimmed shields shone in the morning sunlight, and he easily picked out the red-cloaked centurion, with his silver chain mail blazing in the early morning light, his helmet topped by blood-red feathers.

Horrified and confused, Lucius froze. His thoughts scrambled for a foothold. What to do? Posing as a Christian brother was probably his best chance, since the Christians were now in good stead with the legions. The emperor had recently switched allegiance from Sol Invictus to the Christian God.

He scrabbled back down the side of the dune and found a knob of flint, from which he knapped a sharp shard. He searched out and cut two flat sections of driftwood, lashing them together with tough reeds to form a rough cross. He plaited grasses into a rope and hung the cross around his neck, hoping the Romani would take him for a wild hermit from a nearby island. He bundled his few clothes into the blanket, tied it with another hastily plaited reed rope, slung it over his shoulders, and started down the dune towards the troops.

"Hoy! You there! Stop!" the burly signifier called out. He called to the cornicer to sound the alarm.

Swallowing terror, Lucius composed his face into a mask of serenity and calmly walked towards the signifier. *Milites* and *tirones* ran at him from every direction, and he soon stood within a circle of soldiers, swords drawn.

"I am a brother from that island." Lucius pointed towards a tiny outcrop towards the west.

"What business do you have here?" the signifier asked.

His lorica musculata gave his torso bulk. He looked larger than life, a kind of walking god. While Lucius reasoned that it was just a bronze chest piece, a more primitive part of his brain felt nothing but dread.

"I am making my way inland, on a ... p-p-pilgrimage to the East," Lucius squeaked.

"He's nothing but a lowly Christian. You can see that by the symbol he wears," said one of the *milites*, spitting on the ground to show his opinion.

The *milite* was a proud follower of Mithras, the soldier's god of light and truth. As far as he was concerned, Christianity was the religion of slaves, even if the emperor had taken a fancy to the exotic new cult. In his mind, this sudden conversion was just another eccentricity of the rich and the powerful.

"Well, we still need men for the *auxilia*," said another.

"He's nothing but a boy!" said the cornicer.

"Boy, what skills do you have?"

"I c-c-can work wood and leather," Lucius offered. He thought of himself and Teilo making the little curach with their own hands.

"Put him to work in the boatyard," barked the signifier, already losing interest in the scrawny young Christian.

"But I am—" Lucius fought to explain.

"You are nothing, and you are nobody." The signifier turned his back and walked off to attend to more pressing matters.

Lucius was led back towards the shoreline. Escape was impossible; he was hemmed in on all sides by armed *milites*. They walked towards the sea, passing a cluster of captive Galli with their hands bound by ropes, sitting forlornly in the sand. One of them looked up at Lucius as he neared the group. He gasped. It was Aurelia.

Lucius tried to edge towards her, but she shook her head silently, saying no. It was too dangerous to speak and hopeless to acknowledge each other.

"What will happen to those poor souls?" Lucius asked one of the *milites*.

"Oh, they will be transported somewhere. That's what they get for ruining the peace. This was a nice, calm province until recently; we had everything under control. Now this! Keeping control of the Galli is like holding a wolf by the ears!" He waved his arm expressively towards the trampled and muddy tents.

"They have embarrassed us and our centurion, Gaius Quintus Aurelius. To save face, we are rounding them all up and sending them to the governor of Hispania Tarraconensis. He always needs slaves for his plantations."

Lucius glanced back once more and saw a line of bound captives being forced onto a ship. Aurelia's group were being pulled to their feet and prepared for transport as well. His knees buckled, but there was nothing he could do. He felt the cold knob of a sword pommel against his spine, herding him forward like a dumb beast.

13

A knot of Syrians labored over a new wooden ship in a secluded inlet around a bend in the shoreline. They were slaves of the Romani who, as highly skilled shipwrights, were a valued and essential part of the *auxilia*. They worked regular hours and were even paid a small sum if they did their tasks particularly well.

Huge cast-iron cauldrons of boiling tar and pine pitch reeked along the rock-ribbed shoreline as a group of men swabbed the boat inside and out with the dark mixture using cloth-wrapped sticks. Another group braided ropes out of hemp and dipped the hemp lines into the tar and pitch to waterproof them. Long black cords of newly tarred rope hung like petrified snakes on a line to dry. Seated on the scree that spilled to the shore was another cluster of men, sewing together large rectangular pieces of linen fabric with tar-soaked hempen thread to make the sail.

"I'm leaving you here. This is your work from now on," said the *milite*, pushing Lucius towards a man who supervised the others.

"I am Ugar," the man said, hailing Lucius with a hand stained black with tar.

"I am Lucius."

"That's a common enough name but a Romani one. How did you end up here? Are you a citizen of Rome?" the man asked. His tone was gruff but friendly.

"I was born on these shores. I am Galli."

The old questions surfaced with that declaration. Unclear about his parentage, any mention of the subject brought the familiar pain to Lucius's heart. The hurt was ever palpable, ever a gaping hole.

"You are very lucky, boy. The Romani must think you have something useful to offer them, otherwise you would have been loaded onto that ship out there and packed off to a silver mine or a plantation," said Ugar, facing the sea.

Another peg-legged Syrian approached, carrying a heavy roll of linen. His wooden leg did not dent his ability to lift weights. He eyed Lucius with curiosity. "It's the hair," he said finally. "They like the blond ones; they fetch a high price in the markets of Rome.

"My name is Tannin," he added. "The ship's name is Marah, named after our merciful Goddess of the Waters. I don't know what the Romani will name her, but she is Marah to us. Don't be afraid to ask me anything!" He smiled and stumped off to deposit the roll of linen with the sail-makers.

"Do you ever try to escape?" Lucius asked Ugar, trying not to reveal his anxiety.

"Of course we've tried. We are men, not sheep," Ugar replied with irritation. "It's hopeless; they have sentries everywhere. How do you think Tannin lost his foot? They cut it off as a warning to all of us."

That night, Lucius lay down, exhausted, in a corner of the oil- and beeswax-soaked leather tent of the ship builders. The rags that made up his bed reeked of the sea, tar, and pine pitch, but he was so tired he hardly noticed. The other men fell quickly to sleep. He could hear their deep, stertorous breathing as his worried thoughts stretched out to Aurelia and her family.

"*Deus meus, ex toto corde paenitet me, omnium meorum peccatorum.* O my God, I am heartily sorry for having offended you. I detest all my sins," he murmured, clutching the little wooden cross.

14

Lucius's face was burned from a week of work in the hot sun, his hands blistered and torn from the unaccustomed manual labor.

"Where do you want this ballast to go?" he asked loudly, addressing anyone within hearing.

He and the others had collected round stones from the surf all week, and now it was time to lay them into the bottom of the little ship. Some of the stones had been shaped further with a mallet to make them into perfect spheres, because round stones were essential. If the ship keeled over in heavy seas, they would roll out easily, thus offering a greater chance of saving the vessel and perhaps the lives of the crew. Lucius had a basketful of these shaped stones on his back and several more in his arms.

Not hearing an answer, Lucius placed the stones into the base of the ribs and then turned around to ask for further instructions. No one was moving. Everyone was gazing intently towards the beach. A chariot approached from a distance, followed by a retinue of six *equites*, each horse and rider adorned with a headdress of white plumes. Two figures stood in the chariot, a lady in a flowing white peplos and *pulla* and a charioteer in feathery scaled armor made of bronze, glinting in the sun.

"Who in the name of Asherah is that?" Tannin asked, slowly lowering a large basketful of stones from his shoulders.

"Oh...my gods, it's Flavia Prima, the wife of Decimus Servius Tiberius, the *legatus legionis* for the whole province!" said Ugar. He flung himself down the wooden ladder to properly greet the lady.

The woman in question was the daughter of a Roman senator and one of six sisters, each named Flavia. She was the eldest, hence "Prima." The chariot pulled to a stop, and one of the *equites* dismounted and approached Ugar.

"My lady Flavia wishes to inspect the...um...boat," said the *eques*. He said the words in a careful monotone, with no expression on his face.

They knew otherwise, of course. The lady was famous for her appetites and was known to visit the camps looking for young men to invite home for a bath, a dinner, and other delights. Her husband, Decimus, was often away on tours of inspection of military garrisons and outposts, affording her ample privacy to entertain soldiers, Greek doctors, handsome slaves, and anyone else who took her fancy. She was famed for her collection of Egyptian pornography, painted on papyrus scrolls.

"Who is that one?" The lady Flavia asked one of the *equites*. Her finger pointed to Lucius as she eyed his blond head with fascination.

"I'll find out." He gave his horse a little kick and trotted to Ugar.

Moments later, Lucius was ushered down from the wooden craft and hauled up to ride behind one of the *equites* to the villa of Decimus Servius Tiberius, overlooking the bay.

"He has no idea what he's in for," said Ugar, shaking his head as the chariot and its retinue disappeared over the dunes.

15

After a restful night, Ethne, Ruadh, and Aífe set out again the next morning. They walked for most of the day until they finally reached the hill overlooking the *rath* of Cadla, Ard-Ri of In Medon. Not much had changed, at least outwardly. The same reddish-brown palisade of tree trunks glowed in the afternoon light as travelers and merchants converged on the *rath*, and the same pall of smoke from the cooking fires hung like a thin veil over the conical roofs of willow-thatch that topped the round stone buildings inside the wooden fence. More warriors patrolled the outer walls than in Crimthann's time. As the three drew closer, they saw severed heads hanging on either side of the gates. Cadla was more of a warrior than a philosopher.

The *nemed*, the sacred enclosure of the Druid built on a low rise within the walls of the *rath*, was still hidden within its familiar circular wall of greenery; a gaudy necklace of elder, hawthorn, and rowan bushes bloomed in their full summer glory. The five roads that led to the Ard-Ri's seat through forest and bog had been recently widened and upgraded to ensure that merchant goods, visitors, and warriors could move freely to and from the *rath* from all the provinces. There was more traffic than they had ever seen before.

"It won't be hard for us to slip in unnoticed with all these people coming and going," said Ruadh.

"We should go straight to the *nemed* and find Gaine. I don't want to be mixed up with any problems at court. If Cadla knew we were here, it would only cause tension and conflict," said Ethne.

They pulled their hoods over their heads and fell in behind a large ox-cart filled with sacks of apples and grain, passing through the gate without incident and then veering off towards the *nemed*. But within a few steps there were guards everywhere.

"Where do you think you're going?" asked a grizzled old warrior who was missing an eye. It was not uncommon for disabled veterans to be given guard duty within the gates of the *rath*; it was an easier assignment than guarding the towns and the coasts.

"We are here to speak with the Ard-Ban-Drui. We have walked from a great distance to seek her advice on a spiritual matter," said Ethne, keeping her eyes cast down, hoping the man would not recognize her.

"I'll have to report this to the Ard-Ri. He likes to keep track of everyone who enters the *nemed*."

"Why should he care if people from the countryside want to visit the old Ard-Ban-Drui?" asked Ruadh evenly, also keeping his gaze firmly on the dirt path. "Surely he has much more important matters to be concerned with."

"She will soon pass over to the other side, and we don't want someone new taking her place," said the guard. "As soon as she's dead, the *Cristaidi* will build a stone church inside the *nemed*, right next to that big old tree."

"The sacred ash?" Ethne's head jerked up, and her eyes met those of the soldier.

Years earlier, when Ethne and Ruadh had left the *nemed*, the *Cristaidi* had chopped down the ancient *bile* of In Medon that stood just outside the gates of the Ard-Ri's *rath* for almost a thousand sun-turnings. It was a desecration she still could not forgive. But the sacred ash had been the focus of Druid rites for the good of the earth and the people for a thousand sun-cycles. It anchored the prosperity of the land.

Oaks and ashes were the only trees that attracted lightning—the attention of the gods—and still survived to flourish. They sent their roots deep into the soil and their branches high into the heavens, bringing messages from the sky gods to the earth and from the earth spirits to the sky, and to all creatures, seen and unseen, that dwelled between. Any insult to such a tree, especially when it had been the focus of sacred ceremony for untold generations, was an affront to the ancestors, the sky gods, and the nature spirits. And to the Druid, these trees were people. To desecrate such a tree was tantamount to murder.

Aífe kept silent during the exchange. She had been too young when the Druid escaped into the forest to fully understand all that had been lost, and she did not remember the elaborate rites within the *nemed* nor the respect that had once been shown to the Druid at court.

Ruadh gestured to Ethne to stay silent. In dealings with the *Cristaidi*, it was better for a man to appear to be in charge. That was their way.

"We are not here to cause any trouble," Ruadh said. "We just want to speak with the Ard-Ban-Drui while we still can. We are simple forest dwellers who have need of spiritual guidance."

The guard finally relented. They were allowed to enter the *nemed* but were followed right up to the entrance, where two guards were posted to monitor their comings and goings.

Ethne's expert eye noticed the spreading weeds in the garden at the center of the *nemed*, weeds so thick it was hard to tell how many healing worts were left. Hawthorn and rowan saplings sprouted from berries that had fallen and been left to grow wild in the iris beds. One whole section of the garden was taken over by nettles; in the past, these would have been harvested and eaten in very early spring, but now a grossly overgrown nest of them threatened to swamp the garden in a poisonous, stinging tide.

At least the grass was cut. Some intelligent person had put out a sheep on a tether that was fixed to the ground at one end by a large iron spike. The sheep walked within the large circle afforded by the length of the tether and cropped the grass. This arrangement worked well unless the sheep decided to chew the tether, got tangled in the line, or somehow managed to get into the flower gardens and medicinal shrubs.

Where the Cauldron of the Sea had once stood, a small bronze vessel now sat beneath the sacred ash to receive offerings and to be used for scrying. The fire altar was cold. Nothing but a thin layer of damp black cinders remained of its former glory. Ethne walked to it and said a little prayer. Out of habit, her fingers reached under the round shelf of stone upon which the altar was built to see if the bell branch was still there. She drew back her hand with a start, then reached in again. It was still there!

Ethne took out the branch and shook it experimentally. It sounded just as sweet as it had so many years before. She shook it in a regular rhythm, walking slowly *dessel* around the circumference of the ritual site. The sound of the bells purified the atmosphere and dispelled any lingering negative energies. The sweet sound was a favorite of the fairies and a signal to them that they were still welcome in that place. When Ethne had circumambulated the space three times, Aífe stepped forward, and, to Ethne's delight, began the ancient invocation to the spirits of the land:

Powers of the east, power of the salmon,
Powers of earth and prosperity, come into this space,
Be with us now!

Turning to the south she intoned:

Powers of the south, great sow,
You who delve deeply into the dark earth
To gain her secrets, powers of water,
Of song, of poetry and arts, be with us now!

Turning again, she faced the west:

Great stag of knowledge, power of air,
Power of the west! Be with us in this circle,
Guardian of teaching and learning,
Of history and storytelling, be with us now!

Turning one more time to face the north, she sang out:

Powers of the north, great eagle,
Lord of battle magic, power of light and fire,
From the place where the sun never sets, be with us now!

Then she stepped up to the fire altar, the center of the *nemed*'s holiest sanctuary, and said:

Great horse of sovereignty, mare of the land,
Ruler of kings and queens, be with us here in this circle.
Bring us self-mastery and steadfast judgment, true-seeing and balance.
Be with us now!

Ruadh and Ethne waited for her to finish, moved to tears by the memory of what had once been and was no more. At the end, Ethne removed a small silver phial from her pack and poured a thin stream of the Waters of Life in a circle upon the cold ashes, recalling the dancing flames of long ago.

At that moment a young Drui appeared, a tall, brown-haired man in a white woolen tunic, carrying a stout oaken staff. He appeared to be the gatekeeper for the Druid of the *nemed*.

"I see that you are followers of the Old Way. Welcome to the sanctuary of the gods. My name is Nuin. May I offer you the hospitality of this place?" he asked politely.

"We are here to visit Gaine. That is our only request," replied Ethne.

The young man sighed. "I fear that the Ard-Ban-Drui is very frail. She has not received visitors for some time now."

"She will want to see us," Ethne replied. "Tell her that Ethne and Ruadh are here."

The man looked startled, then bowed slightly in response. He had heard the tales of Ethne of the Forest. He hitched his tunic, took up his staff, and walked as fast as he was able to Gaine's house to announce the visitors.

Word quickly spread that no ordinary visitors had arrived. Some remembered Ethne and Ruadh, and some had heard the stories. Everyone was anxious to meet the former Ard-Rígain and her warrior-poet husband. Aífe was petted and admired by all. A few had known her in her infancy and marveled that she had grown so tall and healthy, and that she was a trained Drui as well. The visitors gave them hope.

Aífe was excited at the prospect of meeting the venerable Ard-Ban-Drui. She imagined sitting at Gaine's feet and memorizing ancient lore directly from her lips.

They entered Gaine's round house and found it filled with light. Beeswax candles flickered in their honor, and a tray of *mid* in a silver flagon and silver cups had been set out for their refreshment. These gestures were reminders of the generosity and graciousness that had always been a part of this community. As they moved farther into the room, they saw the pallet where Gaine lay. Ethne stepped to her side and knelt.

"Gaine," she whispered, and the name caught in her throat and tears came. Not until she saw the dear face and put her hand on the dry, thin hand that lay above the cover did Ethne know how deeply she had missed her old friend.

"Ethne, these eyes have longed to rest on you," Gaine said, in a voice hoary as the winter wind.

She is thin, Ethne thought. *Too thin.* She saw the long grey locks spread haphazardly on her pillow, so different from the intricate braids Gaine had worn all her life. But Gaine was suffused with joy at the sight of Ethne and the others.

"You've come home at last!" Gaine said, beaming.

"Yes, this is one of my homes. You are my home." Ethne bent her head and kissed Gaine's hand, hiding her tears. "Mother, Ruadh and I cannot stay. But we did bring you a gift." Ethne turned and nodded at Aífe to come forward.

Gaine's eyes lit with remembrance. "Ah! The little child of light! How beautiful she is."

"We ask that she stay here with you and the other Druid, if you will give permission. She is a very talented scholar and seer with a true thirst for wisdom. She should be trained as a *ban-fili*," said Ethne.

The light in Gaine's eyes dimmed. "I am afraid that won't be possible. The *nemed* is barely used. The guards come when we light a fire."

"Why?" The knot that had been in Ethne's stomach since they arrived grew tighter.

"Cadla has declared the fire altar a hazard that threatens the other buildings of the *rath*. The cauldron we have is nearly too small for visioning, and the sacred ash gets fewer and fewer offerings from the people. I can feel the land spirits leaving this place. I foresee many sun-cycles of hardship ahead…" Gaine's eyes filled with inner sight.

"This cannot happen. We must keep the ancient teachings alive!" Ethne was overwhelmed with pain and rage. She had been counting on the Druid of the *nemed* to hold the teachings for the future. She needed to know that others held the future of the Drui. She couldn't bear the burden alone; it was too large. There was so much she didn't know.

"There is a place…" Gaine wheezed, and Aífe moved forward to offer her a bit of water.

"Where?" asked Ruadh, ever prepared to take Ethne and Aífe to the ends of the earth and protect them with his life.

"First ask the young ones to leave this house. It is a sacred place…a place of many secrets."

All except for Ethne and Ruadh left the hut, and the leather door was shut. Gaine sat up, looking suddenly alert, and spoke. "There is an island in the north called Innis nan Druidneach by some; others call it Innis Ibrach. You must send her there. To reach it, she will have to take a coracle from the northern shore of Irardacht, from the bay where An Daghda's son Aedh is buried. Take her out beyond the ninth wave, and leave her in the ocean without oars. Ignore her cries; she will think she is lost, but the summer currents will carry her without fail to the southern tip of the island."

"We cannot leave her to the vagaries of the sea! What if there is a storm?" asked Ruadh.

Gaine shrugged, and her eyes looked hard. "Then she will die. Her fate is for the gods to decide."

Ethne sank back, stunned. The greatest Druid, the sun kings, offered their lives for the good of the land and the tribes. To die in the midst of a sacred quest was not a tragedy, it was a high honor. But to send Aífe out alone, without knowing what terror or suffering she would meet, was more than she could bear. Ruadh placed his hand on Ethne's shoulder to comfort her.

"It is ever the way of the Druid to be tested, for learning is the foundation of every poet. She must go, for the good of us all," he said quietly.

Ethne knew the truth of his words. They had given Aífe all that they could; it was time for others to complete her training.

"Bring her to me now. She and I will share this evening. It is the only preparation I can give."

Ethne and Ruadh did as Gaine asked. But as Ethne walked away from the hut, she was overcome with the desire to run, to run and take Aífe away from that small, deceptively safe room.

Inside, Gaine lay for a moment with her eyes closed as Aífe waited. Finally, as if she had gathered enough strength, she opened her eyes and began. "I am told that you have the gifts of the *fili*; can you tell me what you have learned of the poet's art?"

"I have learned the *imbas forosnai*," the girl answered. "They ask me a question and then give me a bit of raw flesh to chew. I place it on the stone that we use for an altar at the Forest School. I sing a song to the gods and go to sleep with my palms against my face. When I wake, I am able to answer the question."

"Go on," Gaine urged.

"I have also learned Teinm Laegda; I know how to put my thumb on my mouth and chant to go into trance. I am able to divine an answer that way too.

"I know the Ogum letters, of course, as both written and sign language. And I can use my fingertips to make a verse or a prophecy."

"And have you the art of satire?"

"Oh, yes, though Ethne told me to be very careful about when and how I use it. We have an ancient hawthorn tree at the Forest School. I

70

know how to stand under it and chant a satire while holding a poppet pierced with thorns. It is a deadly art, I know. Ethne says that all magic returns nine times to the sender, so this kind of magic should only be used if there is no other way. No intelligent person should ever take such a spell lightly."

"She has taught you well," said Gaine. "And do you have the stories?"

"Yes. I know three each of destructions, cow-spoils, courtships, battles, *immrama*, violent deaths, elopements, conflagrations, visions, loves, hostings, migrations, and violent eruptions." She counted them off on her fingers as she spoke, so as not to forget any of the categories of tales. "These I recite only between Samain and Beltaine, at night, in front of the fire. Of course, if there is an emergency, I will recite at other times too.

"I know several forms of composition, and rhymes and meters to make poems. But Ethne always says that the content of prophecy is more significant than elegant wordplay."

Gaine nodded, well pleased that the education in the Forest School was thorough. She was impressed by Aífe's earnest diligence.

"You know a great deal," she said to Aífe. "And you hold the learning firmly in your heart. You will need this faith, and you will need this belief in your own connection to the gods. Remember, child: no one speaks to the gods for you better than you do yourself. Always trust your own knowledge and trust the love you have for those who hold you in their hearts."

Something in Gaine's words made Aífe listen more intently. Something in her voice made her tremble.

"When you doubt the people who love you, you doubt the old ways. Believing in them is the same as believing in the forest, the rivers, the rain, the deep earth beneath you." Gaine reached beneath the coverings and pulled a round stone from a pouch. "When you have no more hope, when all seems lost, close your fingers over this stone. It is the heart of the earth, of this place. It is the center of us all." Gaine closed her eyes.

Aífe sat and waited, sure that there must be more. But there was no more. Gaine was asleep, her soft breathing the only sound in the little room. Aífe stood and quietly let herself out.

The next morning, Ruadh helped Gaine from her bed to a bench in the herb garden, where Ethne plaited her hair and wove lavender blossoms into the braids. They spent several happy days in the *nemed*, weeding the garden and sitting in the sun as they told Gaine and the others about the progress of the Forest School.

Ethne asked how things had fared in her absence from court.

"We have learned to adapt," said Gaine with a faraway look. "We can no longer be open about the Old Gods, so we weave our teachings into stories. We always begin by saying something like: 'It was a belief in heathen times' or 'It is just an old woman's foolishness,' and then we tell a story with the old wisdom hidden inside it. Sometimes I even say: 'This story has been ascribed to demons,' and then I go on to praise those who have memorized it.

"Even the *Cristaide* have taken to learning our stories. I think they realize that the people will not respect them as equals of the Druid, as people of true learning, unless they know about our gods and our teachings.

"They have even started to capture our stories on vellum, of which I do not approve. Capturing the stories means that they can be read or spoken to anyone at any time, and they lose their special power. Some stories should only be told on very rare occasions in a sacred setting. But there isn't much we can do about that."

During the entire visit, neither Cadla nor his soldiers bothered Ethne or Ruadh, thinking the humble visitors too insignificant to merit their attention.

16

The chariot and horses came to a stop at the Villa Candida, so named for its vast length of whitewashed walls that stretched in a square facing the ocean. The rectangular villa itself was built within the walls on a rise so that the inhabitants could see the sea from the portico. The center courtyard of the villa held an immaculately kept garden, filled with rare flowers and fruit trees imported from Egypt and Rome, and three large fountains.

The villa was huge, luxurious even by Roman standards. It had under-floor heating vents where hot air from a furnace was kept circulating by slaves who labored day and night, from fall to spring, by constantly feeding wood to the fires. Running water was piped in from a stream, channeled down from the hills through a miniature aqueduct into three large baths, each with colorful mosaic floors. Two of the bath's floors featured marine scenes of tritons, mermaids, and the god Neptune; one showed a circle of bathing beauties in tiny bathing suits surrounded by dolphins.

The *caldarium* and *tepidarium* faced the afternoon sun to help keep the waters warm through the night. The *frigidarium* was in full shade by noon. A *laconium* was used to sweat out illnesses and for pleasure, and the palaestra allowed Decimus to keep in shape by providing a space to throw the discus and lift weights.

Five bedrooms, a huge formal dining room, a kitchen, and a temple formed the main living area within the villa. Each bedroom was equipped with its own marble latrine, beneath which a constant flow of cold water carried wastes to the sea through a ceramic pipe.

Within the walls was a smaller villa, the Villa Rustica, which housed slaves; horses; a hospital; a storeroom for amphorae of oil, wine, olives, and grain; a laundry; and a prison. It had a barn for goats and chickens and another detached outbuilding that was a staff kitchen.

Decimus had established a flourishing side business shipping slaves to Hispania Baetica and bringing back olive oil, which he then sold to the Roman troops in Germania for a fabulous profit. The prison in the Villa Rustica often held the slaves until they numbered enough to fill a ship.

Lucius stared in disbelief as they waited for the large oaken gates to swing open.

"You'd better shut your trap before the flies get in," said one of the horsemen. The others snickered. They took Lucius for an ignorant country boy and thought he would make a fine toy for their lady.

The chariot stopped before the portico of the Villa Candida and deposited its mistress onto a mosaic that depicted a black puppy barking against a white background. "Cave Canum" was written in black tiles across the top of the mosaic. This deposition was immediately followed by a swarm of yapping and barking fluffballs, who assaulted their mistress with delirious joy. None was bigger than a rabbit.

"Ferox, Lupa, Theron, Tigris! Down!" Flavia screamed, until a slave ran up to relieve her of the maelstrom.

She did not have to issue orders; this was a well-rehearsed routine. Lucius was shoved to the ground in front of the door and left there, wondering what was expected of him, until a slave finally approached and took him by the elbow, saying, "Come this way; you will want a bath," in a tone that did not invite contradiction.

Lucius was led to a small chamber beside the baths and ordered to remove his clothes. The house slave took them away, clearly disgusted and holding the reeking toga at arm's length as he bore it to the rubbish fire. Another slave handed him a soft woolen towel and a pair of leather sandals.

"Do you wish to start with the *caldarium* or with the *tepidarium*?" the second slave inquired. His mouth was slightly pursed, and he looked to the side of Lucius, not at him.

Lucius, offered no indication, tried, "I'll do whatever is usual."

He was led to the *caldarium*, where Flavia was immersed, clothed only in her flowing red hair. Lounging serenely against a wall and clutching a glass of cold honey-wine, she purred, "Come on in, the water is delicious." Her eyes were hungry.

He clutched the towel around his middle. It was clear that the woman thought herself irresistible, but to Lucius her nakedness was shocking, brazen. She looked exactly like the demons that he had heard about in the *schola* at Inissi Leuca. His eyes found the floor; he could not bear to look directly at her.

"Have you never had a hot bath? It won't hurt. Afterwards I will rub oil onto your sunburn. Tsk! Those poor hands! Let me see them." She put down the glass and glided over, took one of his hands, and pulled him into the pool. Once he was in, she stood very close to him and held his hand to her mouth, kissing the palm.

"Do you feel better now?" she asked, batting her eyes slightly.

"No! Yes!" he stammered, sidling back towards the steps.

She watched his hesitation, his confusion. "There's no hurry," she said silkily. "I'll stay here. Lower yourself into the water." She nodded at him.

Lucius felt wary, put off by such flagrant lewdness, but he gradually let himself sink into the warm water, feeling it envelop his sore muscles and aching limbs. The water was like drifting into dream without sleep. He let out a long sigh and a small moan.

She half-closed her eyes and watched him get lost in the feeling, leaning against the marble wall and letting her legs float loosely beneath her.

Lucius sank deeper, closed his eyes, and let the water rise over his chest, his shoulders. He lifted his feet, tilted his head back, and let the water hold him. It was like nothing he had ever known. The cold waters of the ocean and of the streams where he had washed and swum were like playful slaps. This was like swimming in hot tea.

She giggled, and he stood up with a splash. Her eyes pinned him, and all the comfort was gone. He stood half out of the water like a rabbit caught in a clearing.

"Go," she said, somewhat sternly. "You have soaked long enough."

As he climbed out of the pool, she admired the smooth, taut skin of his buttocks as he walked towards the dressing room. She ran her eyes appraisingly over the length of his legs, the shape of his arms.

That evening, after Lucius was massaged, oiled, and dressed in a snowy white toga, he was led into the dining room, where Flavia reclined on a red couch. He had never seen anything like it; all the furniture in the room was gilded with gold leaf, and twenty fat candles flickered at once.

He sat where she indicated on the adjacent couch, and she took his hand and gently caressed it.

"Where are you from?" she purred.

Her breasts were near fully exposed by the low-cut gown she was wearing, and Lucius was becoming flushed with embarrassment—and, he was ashamed to realize, an unwelcome desire.

"I am Galli, from Inissi Leuca. I was taken by mistake. I am not a slave!"

"No?" She gave a little laugh and smiled. "That's a mistake I'm glad someone made."

"I am a Christian brother. I can read and write."

"Ah, a philosopher. A learned man. There are many things I would like you to teach me. Shall I tell you about the god I adore?"

"Which god is that?" he asked, his voice suddenly high pitched.

"Pan. Do you know him?"

"No, lady. I know only my one god."

"One god is not enough." She drew her finger along the line of his jaw. "Not for all the pleasures that we can have. Pan is my favorite god; he is the Greek god of orgies. He can split himself into multiple bodies to ravish many maidens all at once! He gives lovers their fire and their strength." Her eyes glowed.

Lucius pushed her hand from his face. "I am a man of God," he said.

Flavia sat up on the couch and studied his face. She could not tell if he was truly ignorant or if he was just playing a coy game, prolonging the act of pleasing her. She was intrigued. "Come," she commanded abruptly. "Let us eat."

As the night wore on, there were salads, fish, game, figs, and sweets. For Lucius, the sheer volume of food was overwhelming, an overload of the senses. While Flavia was far more interested in the man before her than any food, she let Lucius ply her with questions. She patiently told him the names and natures of the local gods and of the gods and goddesses that protected the door and the threshold. Finally, he asked for the full history of the vestal virgins. *Now we are getting somewhere,* she thought and rose to demonstrate a ritual in the hearth.

"I honor the vestals as I must, as all good Romans do, but my favorite goddess is Venus-Aphrodite."

She reached for a box on a low table near to the fire that was covered in red satin, opened it, and took out a handful of dried red rose petals that were heavily scented with rose oil. She held them briefly in her hands before dropping them slowly onto the flames. As the petals turned to black embers and smoke, she spoke an invocation:

"Golden Aphrodite, born of the sea,
You who travel with grey wolves
And bright-eyed lions,
You who travel with the swift roe-deer
And make them to lie down
Two by two in shady glens,
Bring to me that which I desire . . ."

Lucius thought with a pang of Aurelia, and of her grace and charm that had so easily enticed him. He recalled that when he was near her, when he touched her, it was as if he were melting into a second self, a magical extension of his own form. He recalled her laughter and the simple joy of being with her family.

This woman was completely different. Where Aurelia was gentle and self-effacing, respectful of his wants, this woman was simply obscene. He wanted no part of her. His mind raced to think of ways to thwart her plans.

As she turned to approach the couch and before she could straddle his lap as she clearly intended, he asked yet another intellectual question to throw off her plans. "Please explain to me the concept of the numen. Christians teach that God lies outside of creation, in heaven. But your religion posits that all things are inhabited by a divine essence. Can you illuminate this idea?"

"What?" She leaned away from him, incredulous.

"The numen. If all things contain the divine essence, then are all creatures equal? Are crickets and birds equal to men? Are slaves the equals of a lady such as yourself?"

Flavia searched his face for insult, for a sign that he was mocking her, but she saw none. "Oh," she said, a sudden realization coming over her. "You prefer men, or is it boys?"

Lucius shook his head, confused.

"I can watch," she offered. "We don't need to be alone."

"No, I'm not...that's not...I mean, I can't..."

"Not? Can't?" She reached between his legs and stroked him. His revulsion overrode everything; his body did not react.

She slapped his face hard. She slapped it again. "Eunuch!" she screamed. "How dare you insult me?" She hit at him again and again. "Get out! Get out!"

Lucius fled. A goblet landed on the tiles behind him, and then a plate smashed into the wall near his head. He found the door and ran right into the chest of a burly guard. "Take him to the storerooms!" came Flavia's order through the doorway.

He was unceremoniously ushered into a storage chamber in the Villa Rustica to spend the night. He pushed together a few grain sacks to make a bed and fell into a fitful sleep.

The slaves had never seen a man refuse their mistress, and they were amused.

"Hah!" said the chef, an educated Greek. "Lady Flavia likes to say her slaves are nothing but 'vocal agricultural implements.' I wonder what she'll call this one!"

The next morning, a slave appeared in the storeroom, sent by the cook to collect an amphora of olive oil. Seeing that Lucius was awake, the man first made sure he had his attention and then tentatively drew a design on the dirt floor with his foot.

Lucius watched silently, rubbing the sleep out of his eyes.

The man found a broom propped against the wall and turned it upside down, using the point of the handle to more clearly inscribe the message. It was a fish. The man looked at Lucius to see if he understood, then pointed from the fish to Lucius. At first, Lucius was puzzled, but suddenly comprehension came. "Oh!" said Lucius. "Yes, I too am a Christian." He nodded his head vigorously.

"I thought so," said the man, relief showing on his face. To reveal that one was a Christian in a Pagan Roman house could mean a sentence of death, as he knew from bitter experience. He had lost family members to the circuses.

"No one has ever refused the Lady Flavia. You faced a lioness!"

"Can you help me?" Lucius asked. "I need to get out of here!"

"Yes, I think I can, if you can but wait until nightfall."

Flavia did not send for Lucius that day, nor did she send him food or drink. For her, he no longer existed.

The slave who was named Asbolos because his job was to keep the furnace going and so he was perpetually covered with soot brought bread and water from his own ration. That night, he unlocked the storeroom and urged Lucius to follow him outside.

"I have a cart to carry rubbish outside the gates from time to time. Get under the trash sacks, and I will wheel you out to the hills beyond the outer wall," he whispered.

"Thanks be to God for your kindness," Lucius responded.

In the dark of the moonless night, Asbolos wheeled Lucius out of the gates and down the hill. Once freed from the villa, Lucius made for the shoreline and swam a short distance out to sea, to avoid the guards. He planned to come ashore only when he reached the spot where the little curach lay hidden in the rocks around the bend, just past the boat builders' beach, not far from the villa.

17

Lucius swam towards the strand, timing his approach so that he rode in on a large wave. He sprinted the short distance to the clutch of rocks and pulled out the boat and oars, working as quickly as he could to clear off the tangle of seaweed and drag it back into the surf. Once in the water, he towed the curach past the line of breakers, hauled himself inside, and rowed furiously out to sea.

As he plied the oars, he reflected on his escape from the Romani. He had in the last few weeks met *Pagani* who were good and loving and others who were a complete mystery. He had been raised at Inissi Leuca by monks and brothers who were kind, and he had also seen the horrible violence wrought by Martinus and his followers. The only conclusion possible was that people were people, wherever you found them and whatever faith they professed.

He had also learned that women liked how he looked and that his body responded to their interest. With Aurelia he had even felt love, he knew that now. He would make a poor monk, he thought. Chastity would never be his vocation.

Then he remembered the couples who came to Inissi Leuca to have their unions blessed. The image pleased him. But if he never found a woman who could join his soul as well as his body, perhaps he would go without. Flavia had offered her body only, and that had not attracted him at all. She had called him a philosopher. Maybe it was true.

But philosophy was not going to help him now. He knew that his situation was becoming desperate. According to the laws of the tribes, he would be a stranger and an outcast on whichever shore he landed, with no rights of protection. To be found by the Romani would be even worse; he could end up as a slave in Hispania.

He was utterly alone, adrift on the huge ocean. Or was he? Some god had protected him thus far. He would have to trust in that. And maybe his own people lived somewhere along the shore. If he prayed hard enough, perhaps God, or Ísu, or some Pagan deity would take pity on him. Maybe by some miracle he would be delivered to his very own tribe. Somehow it seemed worth the risk.

He would not, could not return to the circumscribed security of his childhood home with the monks and brothers. He had seen too many ways of life; he had tasted the wide world; he wanted to find out who he was, where he came from, and where he truly belonged. To go back to Inissi Leuca now would mean defeat; he would surely regret it for the rest of his life. He had simply come too far to turn back.

In the grey pre-dawn light, he saw gannets asleep on the water, bobbling by on the waves, hardly disturbed by his passing. The sight made him realize that he too was very tired and hungry, having eaten only bread and water the day before.

When he was well away from shore, he finally stopped rowing and let the wind and currents do the work, carrying him ever northward. He stowed the oars and pulled out an oiled leather tarp that had been folded into the ribbing to be used as protection against rain and to prevent swamping. He covered the boat with it, making a dark cocoon, and nodded, drifting into sleep. And then he slept.

He woke to the sound of gulls and terns screaming; the birds were massed overhead, driving off a marauding skua. Fulmars circled above in spiral loops, and he knew he must be close to shore. But which shore? Then he looked to the west and saw a dark storm line approaching. Suddenly the birds fled, and instantly all visibility was gone.

He fought panic, convincing himself that the storm was a blessing. The little curach would ride it out like a gull floating upon the waves.

He quickly arranged the oiled tarp to collect rainwater by making a well, and when the tempest hit, he was under the tarp while sweet water collected in the small depression.

"Deo gratias!" he shouted to the wind and the wild sea, and to any spirit or deity that might be listening, knowing he would now have plenty to drink. He was no stranger to hunger; he had fasted for days on Inissi Leuca. He would survive.

18

Cadla the Ard-Ri should have been happy, but he wasn't. He had everything he wished for: the central kingdom of In Medon was secure and reigned supreme over the other kingdoms. His only serious rival was the kingdom of Irardacht. Its new king, Cináed, was strong and ever sought to promote the fortunes of the kingdom of the north. He was a Paganus. But so far, Cadla had kept him in check.

Cadla's wife, Nárbflaith, had borne him sons. Tanaide and Eógan had survived and were even now practicing swordplay in the yard. Nárbflaith had died one sun-cycle before, but Cadla had several concubines to grace his table and warm his bed.

When he was feeling depressed, Cadla turned to his spiritual advisor, Máel Ísu. The old Abbott Germanus, now nearly toothless and very frail, had found in Máel Ísu a protégé in whom he could trust. These days, Germanus left the spiritual education of Cadla and the *flaith* to the priest.

Máel Ísu was an educated man who spoke several languages and devoted himself to learning the stories of the Old Gods and Goddesses, the better to frame his arguments with the *Pagani*. He was a strong voice for the new religion of the island.

Máel Ísu's pet project was to seek out ancient holy wells in every district and reconsecrate them in the name of a *Cristaide* saint. He had been largely successful, with one major exception: the people were unwilling to reconsecrate the holy wells dedicated to Brighid.

"Who shall we call on to heal us?" they asked with terror in their eyes. "Who will bless the flocks and the forge and the plow?"

After much fuming and deliberation, Máel Ísu hit upon a brilliant solution. He rededicated the holy wells in the name of a "Saint" Brighid and told the people of a young religious woman who cared for the sick and those in need of comfort. The people were illiterate and would be none the wiser; he would rewrite history to bind these simple people to his faith.

"Máel Ísu!" Cadla called out after the assembly in the Great Hall, beckoning the priest to his side. He whispered into the priest's ear so that no one else would hear. "I feel a sadness coming on me again. In the old days, I always had something to look forward to, something to fight for. Now my life is settled, and I am drifting like a coracle upon the waves. What should I do?"

The priest considered Cadla's options. He was a king. He was rich. He was powerful. He had his health. He had women and dogs and horses. He had sons.

"The devil is tempting you again, that's all. You should be happy. Say fifteen Pater Nosters and reflect on all that you have been given. Make a donation towards the construction of the new chapel that will be built inside the *nemed* once the old witch is gone."

Cadla did these things, but he still felt empty. He sought out Lorcan, an old warrior from the days of his youth in whom he could confide.

"When I was younger and I felt like this, I would practice swordplay or go hunting. If that didn't work, I would go into the forest. I would sit by an ancient oak and listen to the voice of the leaves or find a rock near a stream and hear the song of the waters. Sometimes I would see an eagle or a deer or some other creature, and it would remind me that I too am part of all things, connected to life, to creation. I would feel humble and happy. That is what the Druid taught me to do to refresh my spirit. Then I could return to the people.

"Now Máel Ísu is my Drui, and he says that I may not do those things—he says they are dangerous temptations from the devil. I am supposed to think of the god that is in heaven, ignore the earth's creatures, and look forward to death!" Cadla complained.

"Their stories about a heavenly kingdom sounded nice when we first heard them, didn't they?" Lorcan responded wistfully.

Lorcan especially missed the singing and dancing around the huge fires on festival nights. Sometimes he climbed the ramparts just to watch the distant bonfires on the eve of the fire festivals, imagining the food and the celebrations. The *flaith* could not be seen at the fires, for they were all nominally *Cristaidi* now and had an image to protect. But he sorely missed the wild joys of the old days.

19

As if in response to Cadla's mood, the weather shifted suddenly. Endless rain set in, and the warriors found they could no longer practice in the courtyard, needing to keep their weapons from the damp. Everyone crowded indoors, the *flaith* and warriors into the great round hall of the Ard-Ri, and the slaves and craftspeople into the barns and outbuildings.

The dominant smells at court were now soggy wool, wet dog, and smoldering brazier, interspersed with wet wood as rain leaked down the giant roof-trees. The central firepit hissed continuously as fat raindrops splattered on the burning logs.

"It's as crowded as midwinter in here," said Cadla, feeling gloomier than ever.

Two days later, a messenger arrived from the north bringing news of battle and a serious challenge from Irardacht. Cadla's forces had been severely tested, though they had won in the end. Now, some wounded, they were making their way back to the Ard-Ri's *rath*.

On hearing the news, Ethne and Aife deliberated. As professional healers, they felt a strong duty to help the injured warriors. But they wished to avoid the political firestorm that their presence could ignite.

"You are *liaig*, dedicated to the gods. That is your sacred function, and you cannot refuse to honor it!" said Gaine. "Wear my old tunics.

With hoods pulled down over your faces, no one will recognize you. No one will suspect."

So, dressed in tattered old brown and grey robes, Ethne, Aífe, and a few assistants went to the storehouse of the *rath* where the herbs and other medicines were kept. It was neat and clean—the Druid had seen to that—but the supply of healing worts was paltry, a fraction of what had been there when Ethne had kept inventory.

"We will have to make do. Take vervain, figwort, and oak bark from the shelves. We'll make a strong oak bark brew to wash the wounds, and we'll need comfrey poultices day and night," Ethne ordered.

Several of the Druid set to work putting water to boil and preparing the wound wash. Others went to the *nemed* garden to gather comfrey and plantain leaves and roots to mash with mortars and pestles and spread on linen cloths. Others peeled cloves of garlic, mashed them to a paste, and mixed them with honey to spread on bandages.

Ethne and Aífe soaked flaxen thread and iron needles in a bowl of the sacred liquid called the Waters of Life. No one knew why, but if they performed this ritual, the wounds always healed better. They soaked dried vervain and figwort leaves in hot water to soften them and spread them on bandages. They made a brew of vervain leaves that was bitter to the taste but purifying for the blood.

"Better mix this with elderberries and honey or they will never get it down," said Ethne, speaking from long experience.

When the preparations were complete, the Druid presented themselves at court. They stood at the far end of the hall with heads bowed, hands tucked away in their sleeves.

Máel Ísu saw them enter and became very still as indignation rose in his throat. "We don't need these beggar-poets, these bandits and whores in this place! I don't want them or their filthy potions!"

Cadla was embarrassed and secretly ashamed at the outburst. As Ard-Ri, it was his duty to extend sacred hospitality to everyone who came into the *rath*. He lived by the old maxim *Inhospitality will destroy the flowers.* He understood well, even though the *Cristaidi* said it was nonsense, that the justice and behavior of the king affected the health of the cows, the height of the grain, the weather, even the number of fish in the streams. So the Druid had always taught, and he was loathe to break with the ancient wisdom.

"I am sure the Druid will take care of the injured in their enclosure. You won't have to endure their presence here for long," Cadla said diplomatically, hoping to mollify Máel Ísu.

Nuin was spokesman for the Druid. "We can examine them as they arrive, to see which ones can be safely left here in the hall and which need more intensive care. The gravely wounded will be taken to the *nemed* for nursing."

Máel Ísu grimaced but waved the back of his hand at them as if to say, "Go on, then, do what you must."

The wounded came in gradually, by twos and threes, and Ethne and Aífe supervised the triage. Despite Máel Ísu's protest, Cadla was grateful for the swift and efficient work of the healers and watched with concern as they attended to each warrior. He made a point of thanking each warrior personally for his service to In Medon.

The Druid labored into the night, caring for the injured and carrying or helping the worst cases to the House of Healing within the *nemed*. Ethne and Ruadh kept their heads down and their hoods in place, but Aífe was a stranger to the ways of court and more careless about revealing her identity.

As the last patient settled in, Cadla called for a feast to refresh the Druid and the warriors who were well enough to attend.

"The matter of the feast is delicate," he confided to Lorcan. "Protocol dictates that the highest-ranking person sits next to me, the king, and then all others in descending order of rank. The first cup of liquor must be sipped first by me, then the highest-ranking guest, and then all others. Similarly with the food; I am to be served first, then the highest-ranking guest, and so on. But who gets the first drink after me? The best cut of meat? Máel Ísu or Gaine?"

It was in times like these that Cadla wished he had a Drui at his side, in the manner of the old days. Then he could be sure of justice, precedent, and the proper rules of conduct.

Gaine hobbled to the hall to watch the Druid at work, her right as the most senior Drui. Máel Ísu was livid when he saw her and made a point of taking Cadla by the arm, saying, "It is written that thou shall not suffer a witch to live!"

"She isn't a witch," Cadla replied. "She is a very old lady and the Ard-Ban-Drui."

Cadla had a strong impression that Máel Ísu was jealous of Gaine and the respect that still fell on her like a rich cloak. He seemed threatened whenever she was shown favor, rare as that was. The Druid had worked long and hard, and Gaine deserved the credit, so Cadla finally decided to place Gaine at his side for the feast. Máel Ísu was beside himself.

"I will not partake of this she-devil's feast!" he said, storming out of the hall.

Cadla turned away to keep from showing his irritation. It was then that he noticed Aífe.

She was heedless of everything but the work before her. Her hood had fallen down, and golden ringlets spilled over the neck of the old tunic she was wearing. For Cadla, it was as if the morning sun had broken over a cold, grey sea. For a moment, he stood transfixed, staring.

"Who is that?" he whispered urgently to Gaine as the slaves began to distribute wooden platters of roasted salmon, watercress salad, and barley bread.

Gaine's heart sank, knowing that no good could possibly come of his interest. Hadn't she demanded that Aífe, Ruadh, and Ethne take care to hide their identities and keep their faces hidden? Why hadn't the foolish girl paid more attention? And she a trained Drui! Hadn't she said to Aífe, "Avoid battle, and it will avoid you"?

She leaned casually towards Cadla. "She is no one. A lowly girl—you would find her unrefined. She is a peasant and has no conversation."

But Cadla's eyes gathered her in. "I think you are wrong. She is the loveliest thing that has entered this hall in a decade of summers!" At that very moment, something bloomed in his heart. The grey gloom of his yesterdays was suddenly gone, and the flesh on his bones came alive. A song thrummed in his blood, filling him with bright fire.

"Here!" he said loudly, and all turned to see. He called for the ritual bowl of *fion*, stood, and offered Aífe the first drink. As he presented the bowl, he looked into Aífe's impossibly green eyes and was instantly lost to all reason.

"You are like starlight in a black night. You are like the dawn of a spring morning," he said with a bow, handing her the ceremonial liquid that he should have sipped first, then passed to Gaine, in deference to her rank.

The silence around the table was stiff with shock. Gaine clenched her fists in her lap. *This breach of precedence and hospitality will begin no end of trouble. If we were all warriors, someone in this hall would be dead by now!* thought Gaine. *Why are old men so predictable ... and so foolish?*

No one knew what to do. Embarrassment ran like a jolt around the room. He was an old man of rank; she was so young and so unimportant. But what could they say? He was the Ard-Ri.

Ruadh started to rise, thinking to block the king's absurd action and thus keep him from further disgrace, but Ethne held a firm grip on his thigh, holding him to his seat, thinking it best not to call attention to themselves.

Cadla next invited Aífe to sit next to him, usurping Gaine's position as the most honored guest. Aífe demurred, but Gaine shook her head, indicating that Aífe should be compliant and not cause trouble. It was rare enough that the Druid were invited to the hall of the Ard-Ri and rarer still that they shared his meat. Pride of place meant little to Gaine personally; she could withstand any insult if it helped to bolster the prestige of the Druid.

Silence reigned for the rest of the meal, and Cadla noticed nothing, saving his attention for cutting choice bits of meat and putting them onto Aífe's plate. He watched her eat every morsel as though he were devouring her.

"Who are you?" he finally asked.

"A student in the *nemed*" was all the answer she gave.

"But you are newly arrived?"

Aífe nodded and said, "I have traveled far to be here."

It was all she could bring herself to say. Charmed with her shyness, Cadla let those words suffice ... for the moment.

20

"Now we are trapped here!" Ethne said in dismay to the gathered Druid when they were back in the *nemed*. "He will never let her escape—not unless he loses interest, which I highly doubt."

The morning after the feast, Cadla consulted with his closest advisors, already inquiring about the suitability of taking a new chief wife. The girl was a Drui, a member of the highest rank of society. He began inventing excuses to bring her to court.

"I will personally convert her from her *Pagani* ways. I will bring her to the god Ísu. Máel Ísu will be pleased!"

"I have an injury that needs attention," he would say in the morning.

"I need her to judge a poem I am attempting to compose," he would say in the afternoon.

After she left, he would invent another reason to see her.

"I want her advice on which healing worts to grow in the garden. There is a wonderful new flower that I want her to see."

He invited her for walks outside the gates to pick berries. He told her to open her mouth so he could feed her from his hand. He took her to the ancient stone circle on the hill outside the *rath* and asked her to invoke the Old Gods for his pleasure. She could hardly refuse.

He commissioned cloaks and dresses for her, all of bright colors and costly cloth. He gifted her with amber beads for her neck and golden balls for her hair, insisting that she wear them each night at his table.

When he was alone with her, he could barely keep his hands to himself.

"I haven't felt this way since I was a newly made warrior!" he confided to Lorcan.

Aífe wore layers of clothing and kept her head modestly covered, sidling away each time he stood too close. He found her reluctance charming; it added mystery and fired his ardor to possess her completely.

For Aífe, he was old enough to be her father, and his attentions were revolting.

"You and my father would have been friends, I am sure," she said once when Cadla's hands were trying to find their way under a fold of cloth. "You are so much like my grandfather." But these hints were futile.

Máel Ísu followed Cadla into his bedchamber to admonish him. "Stop chasing after this girl! It is beneath your dignity. Do you remember how the Druid tricked the Ard-Rí, Crimthann, into marrying that Pagan whore Ethne? She had a *fennid* lover right under his nose! Crimthann died a *Pagani* and no doubt went straight to hell. You will too if you don't stop. It's a Druid trick to bait you; they want to pull you and all of In Medon back to their heathen ways. It is obvious they've put a spell of *druidecht* upon you. I fear you are bewitched!"

But Cadla stopped his ears. He had not been this happy for years, and he was not about to give up the girl.

One night, after insisting that Aífe sit beside him at table in the place of honor, at a feast where dignitaries from far and wide were present, Cadla rose to make a speech. "Honored guests, as I raise this bowl of *fíon* to take the first sip, I make a solemn oath. This beautiful golden lady at my side will be my wife at Lugnasad!"

Everyone stood up cheering and congratulating the king until even the dogs under the table barked in chorus. Aífe felt faint and lowered her head. Cadla mistook her pose for modesty.

"This oath, sworn over the ceremonial cup of liquor in the presence of my guests at table, is sacred. This oath has been heard by the gods, and I am willing to die in the fulfillment of it!"

Witness upon witness of noble rank stood about the hall. For Cadla to break his oath would mean a fatal loss of face. It would mean the loss of the kingship.

Cadla beamed down on Aífe. He had bestowed on her the highest possible honor.

Aífe felt sick. This was nothing she wanted nor had ever dreamed of. Riches, fine clothes, and the privileges of queenly rank were simply not in her nature.

"You have the soul of a poet," Ethne used to say to her from the time she was an infant in the Forest School. She was still thirsty to learn from within the ranks of the Druid—the Brehon Laws, the mastery of magic, the ancient philosophy handed down from the ancestors...All this she wanted as if it was the very air she needed. She stood, trying not to show the trembling in her body. "Please excuse me; I must go to the *nemed* to tell them the news."

As soon as she was free of the court, she ran to the *nemed* to find Ethne and Ruadh in Gaine's roundhouse.

"I cannot, will not do this!" Aífe cried, with tears of frustration welling in her eyes.

Ethne remembered her own arranged marriage with Crimthann, the former Ard-Ri, so many summers before. Her heart ached for Aífe's plight.

"I have felt such a dilemma would occur!" said Gaine. "I have thought long and hard about an honorable escape for Aífe."

"How is that possible?" said Aífe. "He has sworn a sacred oath in front of the *flaith*! To let me go would cost too much. I am doomed."

"Your education is not yet complete, my child. There is an answer to this within the ancient tribal laws. He seeks your company by day and by night. It should not be hard to tempt him into some intimacy by simply dropping your guard and letting him catch you. Then you must cry out so that others will hear you, and it will all be over."

"I fully agree," said Ruadh, who stood as foster father to Aífe. She was too valuable to the Forest Druids to be lost like this. Too many sun-seasons had been given to her schooling for her to be trapped as a *Cristaide* warrior's queen. The people needed her, and the land needed her. Of this he was certain.

21

The next day, Cadla found another excuse to invite Aífe to court. "The apple trees are blooming, and I want you to see them. It is a rare sight when they are all in full flower!" He imagined her sitting under the blossoming trees, he bending to her, her head tilting up, stealing a soft kiss. He imagined her sun-warmed body, his breath on her skin, the nearness of her breasts.

"I must dye cloth for Gaine," Aífe said in response.

"Let the slaves do that. Don't stain your hands!"

"There is other work I need to do as well in the *nemed* garden."

"Let the other Druid dirty themselves. You are not meant for such labor."

"I have to help Gaine, she is unwell."

"The others can see to Gaine's welfare. You need not trouble yourself."

Aífe fell silent. She could think of no more excuses. Cadla took her silence for assent and issued orders for an outdoor feast. Aífe knew that a retinue of warrior guards and slaves would witness their activities under the trees.

Food was ordered and a woolen blanket spread on the grass with colorful pillows thrown down to recline upon. Cadla poured a cup of honey-sweetened *fion* and presented it to Aífe, who drank a few sips and smiled shyly. Encouraged, he leaned closer, breathing in the scent of her hair, of her skin. Aífe tilted her head slightly toward him and asked, "Do your duties allow you many hours like this?"

"Nothing in my life has allowed me even a moment like this." Cadla hooked one of her curls with his finger and let the light play on it.

She brought her shoulder up and turned a little toward him. It was a gesture of demure acceptance. Cadla's breath stopped in his chest. He bent to her. She raised her shoulder a fraction more and leaned forward so that her silken shawl slipped off of her shoulder, baring her neck and arm in the sunlight.

Cadla was intoxicated. Bending to kiss the exposed shoulder, his lips brushed her honeyed skin.

Aífe's body jerked and a strangled scream escaped. She jumped to her feet. The warriors, posted at a polite distance, made a hesitant step forward. The slaves dropped their platters.

"What is it?" asked Cadla. "Are you hurt?"

"You have no right!" Aífe cried. "You, a leader, should know!"

"No right?" Cadla's face flushed red. "I have *all* the rights!"

"Is a leader above the law?"

"What are you saying? What injury have I caused?" Cadla was in dismay. His face was now pale, and his fists were clenched. He was angry, stung, and bewildered.

Aífe gathered her loose clothes around her and ran to the *nemed*. Cadla, confused beyond speech, left the orchard, giving no orders to the soldiers or slaves who stood shifting from one foot to the other in uncertainty.

Later that afternoon, Gaine, Nuin, and the other Druid escorted Aífe to the Great Hall of the Ard-Rí. The Druid were dressed in their most formal robes, wearing six-colored cloaks and torcs to announce that this was a serious official matter. Their expressions were somber. Ethne and Ruadh stood in the shadows at the back of the hall with hoods low over their faces, as neophytes too lowly to approach the king would do.

Cadla sat on his carved wooden throne at the end of the hall. The Druid walked to him and stood in a line facing the dais. Gaine stepped forward and shook her chain with the golden bells in the ancient manner. Despite his *Cristaide* pretensions and his anger, Cadla was moved as she intoned the time-honored words to open the assembly: "In the name of the three worlds of the ancestors, nature spirits, and gods, I declare this assembly open."

She banged the floor with her staff three times and formally petitioned the king for justice. "You, Cadla, have done Aífe great wrong. You violated her person in a crude and unforgivable manner. For the laws state 'If a woman makes an assignation with a man to come to her in a bed or behind a bush, the man is not considered guilty even if she screams. If she has not agreed to a meeting, however, he is guilty as soon as she screams.'"

"But she came willingly! All the court heard her," Cadla said.

Aífe filled her mind with courage, thinking of all she might lose—all her sun-turnings of study at the Forest School wasted. Never to learn the higher mysteries of *filidecht* if she were tied to the Ard-Ri. She could not bear it. Finally she found the words.

"I did nothing willingly. Four times you insisted that I join you under the apple trees. I did not want to go with you. I told you four times I would not, but you would not listen. You are the Ard-Ri; I followed your order. In the orchard, you kissed me. Never did I say my permission. Thus you have broken the law."

There was no sound in the room. Cadla stared at Aífe as if for the first time. She had never wanted him, never returned his desire. His old man's heart went cold as he saw that she had joined him at table and on outings only because he had asked her, because he had insisted. She had never responded in kind, had never asked to see him. He saw her dislike and was mortified. He was a fool.

"I have mistaken your beauty for refinement. I was willing to give you the highest honor I can bestow, to make you my *rígain*. I will not force an unwilling, ignorant girl."

"My only desire is to leave this *rath* and finish my Druid studies," Aífe replied, head high, eyes clear and calm.

Cadla was angry, humiliated, embarrassed. With so many witnesses, there was nothing he could say. As a Druí member of the Nemed class, she was his equal, and he had no right to force himself upon her. The ancient tribal law had been invoked, and he was honor-bound to respect it. Yet his pride fought for him.

"Get out of my sight!" he said, rising and turning his back to the gathering of Druid and Gaine. It was an act of disrespect, but the Druid knew it was a small gesture meant only to end his humiliation.

Cadla retired to his private chamber, and the Druid went back to the *nemed*, where Gaine pronounced judgment. "Even a king must bow to the ancient laws and customs. As the poets advise:

> Give two-thirds of your gentleness to women
> And to the attendants who serve you,
> And to the poets who make the songs ...[2]

"Cadla in his confusion has tried to be just. And that is an end to this foolishness."

22

Lucius knew he was heading north because it was still Eqvos, the Horse Month, and the prevailing winds were from the south and southwest. After the storm, the fish rose near the surface and birds reappeared, scooping up meals that glinted silver in the sunlight. A flock of gulls followed the tiny craft.

A dead fish floated by, and he grabbed it. Tearing enough cloth from the hem of his shirt to make a rope, he trailed the fish behind the boat. When a bird went for the fish, he hit it over the head with an oar, fished the dead bird out of the waves, twisted off the head, tore out the feathers, and split the bird's breast with his fingers, removing the entrails. He ate the flesh raw after rinsing it in seawater for the salt flavor.

He noticed that there were puffins. In summer, puffins do not stray far out to sea, keeping close to their nests. He reasoned that he must be near shore and kept his eye on the flocks overhead to determine the direction of land, somewhere to the east.

Suddenly, he was surrounded by thousands of birds; guillemots, razorbills, fulmars, gannets, puffins, and terns circled and screamed overhead. He was near some island or cliff, a nesting site. Strengthened by the flesh he had eaten, he paddled eastward with confidence, arrowing towards an unseen shore.

I feel I am on a mystical voyage to some island in the Otherworld, he thought. He had no idea where he was, but he knew that wherever he landed, he would be a stranger, a person without status, forced to use his wits to survive.

"Ah, well, 'Every smith is entitled to coal, and every cauldron deserves a bone,' as the old saying goes. Every skilled person deserves a fee for his work. I can read and write, and now I even have a little skill at ship building. I will find a way ..."

He said these things out loud to reassure himself that they were true.

Then out of the sea mists a cliff appeared, looming over the waves. As if in answer to his small prayer, he saw people below the cliff. They were building a boat.

23

"ello!" he hailed them loudly in Gaulish, the lingua franca of the entire Celtic world.

They stared in open-mouthed amazement as he slogged onto the beach, dragging his miniscule craft across the sand.

"Where did you come from?" one said.

"Are you man or water spirit?" said another.

A small crowd formed around him, and men reached out to finger his clothes, to see if he was human.

"I am as human as you are," Lucius replied. "Where have I landed?"

"You're in Cornubia," someone said.

Cornubia! He had barely heard of it. He was on the coast of Albu! The smell of ox hides soaking in lime assaulted his nose. He could see the wooden frame of a ship propped high on stones so that workers could get underneath to lash the latticework with leather thongs, like an enormous basket. The men appeared to be native *Pagani*, so he was less afraid than he might have been. At least they weren't Romani.

"I am Galli, from the south. I was blown out to sea, and I have been drifting for some time. May I rest here for a while?"

"We don't see strangers very much. You are welcome to stay and rest as long you like. As you see, we are building a *scatho* on the *carreg*," the man said, pointing.

"Oh, yes, I understand. You are building a boat on the rocks."

It wasn't hard to follow the man's broken Gaulish once it was embellished with hand gestures. He felt the same open-hearted hospitality here that he had experienced amongst Aurelia and her kin.

"I am Hammitt, head man of this tribe. Here is my first wife, Ienipa; my second wife, Karenza; my sons, Merryn and Denzil; my daughters, Elsed, Steren, and Elowen."

They all had the same long, shiny brown hair and wore simple clothing of identical rough weave, design, and color. It seemed that that the women dyed, wove, and sewed their garments communally.

A dizzying number of family introductions followed until Lucius despaired of remembering any of them. When the introductions were complete, the crowd parted respectfully as a proud and dignified elder approached, treading slowly across the sand.

"This is Meraud, the wise-woman of our tribe," said Hammitt.

She was dressed in a leather cape covered with bird feathers, each one tied on individually with bright red thread, and her hair looked as if it had not been combed in many a year, with long clumps of grey hanging down like snakes coiling past her shoulders. There were feathers, stones, bits of metal, and shells woven into the stringy mass. She leaned on a staff with a skull affixed to the top, which by its size and shape appeared to be the head of a female goat or deer. Thin strips of red, black, and white leather hung down from the skull, and a wreath of seasonal flowers and herbs was affixed to the skull's crown.

She looked directly into Lucius's eyes. A current of raw power passed into him such as he had never experienced. When she touched his face with her thin, dry hand, he was instantly transported. No longer was he standing on a beach in Cornubia; he was on a far-distant shore, standing on a high rock in the middle of an island. From the rock, he could see the ocean below in every direction and the land spread around him on every side like a vast green carpet.

This is what a sky god feels like, looking down on the people, he thought.

She removed her fingers from his face and he was just Lucius again, lost and alone on a beach, in the midst of a tribe of strangers.

The old woman gave him another penetrating look, then murmured some words to Hammitt.

"She says, you will eat your meal with us tonight, and then you will go to the *fogo* of Mamm an Bys and give thanks. Then we will take you to the holy well to visit the Goddess there. You will get a vision."

The only word that made sense was "meal." He was famished.

24

The tribe engulfed Lucius. Skin drums and reed pipes appeared as the people of Mamm an Bys danced and fluted their way up the sandy path to the grassy headland above the cliff. They rarely entertained strangers, and he was a welcome diversion from their usual routine. Laughing and joking, they spoke excitedly to him and to each other along the way. He could not understand a word but was struck again by the happiness on their faces.

There is a mystery here, he thought. *I have never seen so much peace and joy amongst the brothers on Inissi Leuca. What is it that the Pagani have that Christians are missing?*

They brought him to their village of round stone houses overlooking the sea.

"*Mar plek.* Please come in my house," said Hammitt, gesturing Lucius inside.

The house was large, being the home of the head man—so large that the entire tribe could sit comfortably around the rock-rimmed central hearth for a formal meeting or feast. Beds ranged along the walls and covered with grasses and skins also made comfortable benches.

While Hammitt's wives cooked, a storyteller talked, sang, and pantomimed a long seafaring tale. Lucius followed little of it but enjoyed the spectacle, especially as he was clutching a frequently replenished wooden cup of *corma*, made all the more potent by his empty stomach. He joined in the riotous laughter at all the appropriate moments.

When the feast at last appeared, it was served on huge wooden platters that were passed around so everyone could reach in with their bare hands. There were boiled gull's eggs, roasted fish of many kinds, cooked shellfish, dried seaweeds, and fresh puffball mushrooms.

The main course was a huge joint of meat that had been rubbed with mashed wild garlic and sea salt, wrapped in several pounds of moist bread dough, and left smoldering on the embers to cook all day while the tribe worked on the boat. Only the bottom of the dough was charred by the fire, and when the round shell of bread was cracked open, it and the meat within were cooked to perfection.

Lucius quickly learned his first Cornubian expression. *"Meur ras ta* means 'thank you,' the most important words in our language," said Hammitt.

The tribe prepared to sing, tell stories, and drink *corma* all evening. At one point, Meraud appeared and gestured for Lucius to follow her outside. Hammitt was to accompany them as translator. As they left the building, a matronly looking woman handed Lucius a woolen cloak against the damp sea mist.

Their way lit by a single torch, they left the house and plunged into the black of a moonless night. Once again, Lucius felt that he was on an otherworldly quest.

"I am relaxed and full of food, so I might as well enjoy it," he thought as they negotiated the narrow, stony path through the surrounding darkness.

They came to a place even darker than the surrounding night. After a moment of disorientation, Lucius registered that he was standing before a cave. As Meraud spoke and gestured, the shells and stones in her hair clinked softly. Hammitt translated:

"This is the *fogo* of Mamm an Bys, the Earth Mother. Very sacred. Mamm an Bys teaches the people how to grow the grain and how to grind it to make bread. Here we pray our thanks, and here we store food. Here we also hide when enemies come. Come inside, make a prayer."

As they entered the pitch-dark passageway, the single torch guttered, and Lucius saw an altar against the wall. It featured the carved image of a mermaid and a small figure of a bull.

"Who is this altar dedicated to?" he asked.

"That is the altar of Kana'nim. Those people always visit on their way to Ictis Insula for tin trade and come inside the *fogo* of Mamm an Bys to pray their thanks at reaching land. They have gods—El and Baal—and goddesses—Astarte-yam and Asherar-yam. They say Astarte-yam appears as a mermaid. She is also Earth Mother and Sky Mother. Which gods hear you?"

"Oh, who do I pray to?" He was about to say "the one God," as he had been taught on Inissi Leuca, but he realized that this statement was no longer true. His experiences had revealed that there were more gods and more mysteries in the world than he had ever imagined possible.

"I pray to the god of my people ... and I pray to the gods of *your* people," he finally responded.

Meraud's wrinkled old face lit up like a summer's day.

"Yes! This is good! We will go to the holy well!" she said in passable Gaulish, grabbing him excitedly by the sleeve and pulling him back into the soft dark.

"*Meur ras ta,*" he murmured to the guardian spirit who kept watch over the people of Mamm an Bys.

25

Meraud reached into an old leather bag at her side and brought out a handful of dried lavender, some pearly white shells, and a small round of cheese.

"You take. Leave as offering for the spirit of the holy well. Put on the ground. Don't eat!" she said, pressing the objects into Lucius's hands.

They walked for a while in the darkness until they reached a large standing stone, upright and thick as a tree. Lucius heard trickling water nearby. The torchlight revealed a wide fissure in the bare rock, plunging into a deep recess hidden in the land.

"Careful! Very deep!" Meraud said.

"We will leave you here all night," Hammitt added. "Lie on the stone near the well and sleep. Drink water now and again in the morning." He pointed to a leather bucket on a rope that was tethered to a stone.

Lucius had no idea why they wanted him to do this. As a guest in a strange country, he had little choice but to honor their wishes. His survival rested in their hands.

"*Chons da!*" they said in chorus as they disappeared down the slope towards the village.

Now what? Lucius thought.

He dropped the leather bucket into the fissure of rock as he was told, finding that the well was quite deep. He hauled up water and drank a few sips, then set the bucket aside for the morning. He laid the cheese, shells, and herbs at the base of the menhir and lay down on the bare rock as instructed. By pulling up his legs, he curled into a warm cocoon inside the woolen cape, fervently hoping that he wouldn't roll in the night and fall into the water and drown.

It began as a trickling sound, as if a wide and shallow splay of water were rippling over moss-covered stones in a deep forest. Very gradually, the melodious sounds of dripping were added, and then almost imperceptibly the cascade of a waterfall layered in, growing louder and louder. When the water sounds had reached the level of a chorus, the singing started: a perfect three-part harmony in some impossibly beautiful yet indecipherable ancient tongue.

In the midst of all that loveliness, a tiny blue light appeared that gradually intensified and grew in size until it was as long and wide as a human form. The blue light opened like a shell and revealed a molten golden light, within which was the shape of a woman. As the figure took on clarity, breasts appeared, and then long, wavy hair wafted upwards as if the creature were underwater. The lower half of her body was covered in iridescent, luminous scales, tapering into pure energy that swirled below her like an undulating, translucent veil.

Lucius realized with a start that he too was underwater! He too was surrounded by a bright blue light, yet he could breathe easily and speak without drowning.

"Where am I?" he asked. "Who are you?"

The golden woman smiled with pearly luster. Her ocean eyes sparkled with an infinite compassion, as if the whole world were held within them. She reached out her arms, her voice echoing in waves, as if the sound of it were simultaneously near and at a great distance.

"I am called Astarte-yam and Asherar-yam. I am Earth Mother. I am also Sky Mother and Water Mother. I am the spirit who protects the people of Mamm an Bys and all those who sail within and upon the blue oceans. I also protect the creatures of the land and of the sky. I have protected you since the day you were born, even on your island, Inissi Leuca."

Tears of awe and gratitude welled up in his eyes, for he knew that this was true. He had felt her breath upon him like a tender mother, cushioning him from danger and fear. He had always known yet only realized it now.

She continued. "You said 'thank you' just now in the *fogo*, and I heard you. I have a wish for you. Do you want to hear it?"

"I want to hear everything you have to say!"

"Your journey is not over unless you wish it to be. There are more waters to cross and more mysteries ahead if you but choose them."

"I know this is true, lady. There is more for me than this place."

"Go back to your small curach and ride the waves. I will protect you always."

There was so much more he wanted to ask, but the golden form folded into the deep blue light. The light slowly shrank into a tiny blue ball and winked out. The chorus of water sounds silenced, and he was left wide awake on the lip of the well.

The dawn came quickly. "Did you drink water this morning?" Meraud asked gently. "Did you see the water spirit last night?"

"Yes, I did. But she is more than that, much more. She is the mother of all the mountains and of the rivers and of the oceans and the sky!" He said this with awe.

"Yes, yes!" Hammitt and Meraud repeated in chorus, smiling and pleased, nodding their heads.

"Meraud knows you have the connection to spirit. She knew because you traveled alone on the waters without fear. You are a true child of Mamm an Bys," said Hammitt.

"She told me to continue my journey if I want to. I must go," Lucius replied.

"Yes, you must go," said Meraud, placing her hands on his head as a blessing.

26

Ethne, Ruadh, and Aífe set out for Irardacht the morning after their confrontation with Cadla. To help him save face, they did not return to the hall of the Ard-Ri; instead, Gaine sent a messenger to tell him they had gone.

At the gates, Gaine intoned an ancient blessing to protect them in their travels:

"Bless the pathways on which you go,
Bless the earth beneath your soles,
Bless you as you go over the seas
Against drowning, against peril, against spells,
Against wounding, against fright.
Nor brand shall burn thee
Nor arrow rend thee.
You shall go and return triumphant,
As the sun who rises victorious
Above the dark sea of night."

Gaine kissed Aífe's cheek. "Go with joy, my child. The whole world is before you." She turned to Ruadh and embraced him. "May your warrior's heart keep you strong." Lastly, she put her arms around Ethne. "You are the breath of this *nemed*; you are the priestess I would have the Druid follow."

117

Ethne, feeling the fragile bones in her arms, wept as she held Gaine close. "Mother of my childhood, I carry you in my heart as the sun rises and as the moon sails the sky. You live through every word I teach." They held each other close, then Gaine put her hand to Ethne's cheek, pulled herself away, and walked steadily back to the *nemed*.

They traveled in their accustomed way, begging shelter for the night at isolated farmsteads, bartering with tales for their supper. When the weather was fine, Ethne and Aífe foraged for wild greens while Ruadh hunted or fished, then they ate wild game roasted on green sticks and slept around an open fire.

Aífe had no clear idea where they were going or why. Ethne and Ruadh were loathe to tell her the purpose of their journey north until the last moment, to spare her from fear. When she asked, they simply told her to wait and keep silent. Druid-trained, she was patient.

To cover their tracks in case Cadla had second thoughts about vengeance, Ruadh always cut a square of turf and carefully lifted it aside, and then built their fire on the exposed soil. The next morning, he meticulously replaced the turf, leaving no visible trace of their passing. It was an old trick of the *fiana*.

Within a few weeks, they had reached the shores of Loch Feabhail. Ruadh left Aífe with Ethne in a secluded cove and set out to barter for a curach in the settlement nearby. While they waited, Ethne and Aífe settled themselves on the sun-warmed rocks. Ethne knew it was time.

"Aífe, have you heard the tale of Bran, son of Febal, and the Blessed Isle?"

"I have heard the story, but it was many, many sun-turnings ago."

"Then let me refresh your memory. Bran mac Febal was walking out one day beyond the gates of his *rath* when he heard a sweet music that magically put him to sleep. Upon waking, he discovered that he had a silver apple branch in his hand with sprouting silver leaves, fruits, and blossoms. He carried that apple branch back to his *dun*, and the gates were locked behind him.

"When he entered his Great Hall and joined his warriors and their ladies, a strange woman materialized in their midst, singing of Emhain

Abhlach, an isle where there is no sorrow or want. She sang of the white seahorses of Manannán mac Lir that course around its shores and of an ancient tree at its center, ever in flower, filled with singing birds. She sang that it is a place without sickness, suffering, or death; a place without winter; a place of peace, health, and happiness. When her song was done, the apple branch flew out of Bran's hand into the woman's, and then she disappeared."

"She sounds like one of the *Sidhe*," said Aífe in a logical tone.

"Some would say that. Others would say she was a messenger from the Otherworld, describing an island where the dead go in the Western Sea. But what if I told you that such a place actually exists in the mortal world?"

Aífe could see that Ethne wasn't joking, and her eyes grew round in amazement.

At that moment, Ruadh appeared. "I found one, and it is waiting on the shore," he said to Ethne.

"Found what?" Aífe asked.

Ethne and Ruadh looked at each other.

"He has found a curach to take you to sea," said Ethne quietly, holding Aífe's hands to reassure her.

"I don't understand." Aífe looked from one to the other.

"For your safety, but more for the survival of all the Druid, you must go." Ethne kept hold of her hand.

"What about you? You are the keeper of the ancient ways. I cannot go alone."

"No, Aífe, your journey begins here. The gods are calling you. We must stay here and tend to the people. We will go back to the Forest School and teach the children. They have much learning yet before them." Ethne held herself firmly. She could allow no doubt, no grief to turn her aside from setting Aífe on her way.

"No!" Aífe wailed. "You cannot leave me! I will not be away from you!" She clung to Ethne.

Ruadh put his arms around them both and relayed Gaine's instructions. "It is no longer possible for you to finish your Druid training at the *nemed* of the Ard-Ri. Cadla has disgraced himself, and the new religion of the god Ísu has encroached upon the island. We have gone into hiding in the forest just to keep our teachings and traditions alive.

"But there is an island in the north called Innis nan Druidneach by some and Innis Ibrach by others. It is the holiest island of the Druid, reachable only by those specially chosen by the gods. To finish your studies and be a true mistress of *filidecht*, you must go there. There is no other way."

"But alone?" she asked, terror gorging her throat.

"It's the only way. For uncounted sun-cycles it has been so. The elders teach that when a curach is put out to sea from Loch Feabhail in the Eqvos month, the currents and winds will conspire to bring it to that magical place. And to be found worthy, you must go in confidence, without oars."

Aífe stared neither at Ethne nor Ruadh but into some middle space as a sorrowing despair came over her. "You mean to set me adrift beyond the ninth wave like a common criminal. You intend to cast me out in the *cinad ó muir* to meet my death or wash up as a slave on some foreign shore." She shuddered, covering her face with her hands.

The reason for their arduous journey was at last sinking in. Now Aífe understood why Ethne and Ruadh had been so grim and silent. It was beyond imagining.

"Aífe," Ethne began, "we took our lives into our own hands when we left the protection of the *nemed* so many sun-turnings ago. You were too young to realize the courage it took. We were outcasts, courtesy of the *Cristaidi* missionaries who swayed the *flaith* and the Ard-Ri to their beliefs. It's a wonder they didn't come and tear down our school the way they chopped down the sacred trees and destroyed our groves and altars in every district."

"But you had the protection of Ruadh and the *fiana*; you didn't have to stand alone!" Aífe wailed, striving fiercely for self-control. Her teeth were chattering, and she suddenly felt very cold.

"That is so, but you are destined for another fate. The greater the test, the greater the reward. Everything we do now is for the sake of generations to come. All that you have learned, all that you have been given to this moment was passed down to you from those who went before. It is your turn to shine like a star in the dark night. Did you think that all your learning was for yourself alone?"

Aífe pulled her head up and looked directly at Ethne. "No. I carry the stories so that others may know. I am ashamed."

"There is no shame in being frightened," Ruadh said. "The fiercest warrior knows fear before battle. Courage comes from looking past the fear. I have seen you do that." He smiled at Aífe. "Remember your swordplay? Remember how you stood your ground, even against several of the bigger boys? That was courage past fear."

Aífe's eyes filled with tears, but she gave Ruadh a small smile. "I just didn't think I would be called upon to offer my life for the people so soon."

"It's in the hands of the gods whether you will arrive at the Druid Isle. You might wash up on another shore, and then that will be your fate. There is no way to predict. You must be a warrior in this quest," said Ruadh, thinking of the times he had willingly offered his own life's blood for the protection of others.

"A spiritual warrior," added Ethne.

Aífe saw that there was no backing away. She felt transparent, already half a ghost. "I will surrender myself to the will of the gods, the Druid, and the sea."

Ethne grabbed Aífe and held her in a fierce embrace. "You are my daughter, Aífe. You are of me in mind and spirit and heart. Know your strength, for it is great. Know I will never fail in sending you protection." She kissed Aífe's tear-streaming face, her own face wet.

They walked her to the shore and gave her one day's supply of food and water. Aífe climbed into the boat, and they swam the little curach beyond the breakers, setting it adrift. Ethne swam back to shore, then stood in the surf, weeping. The memory of another child lost to the water nearly made her fling herself into the waves to catch Aífe back, but Ruadh held her tight, his own grief beyond speech. They stood in the cold shallows, watching, until the tiny vessel floated out of sight.

27

The first day, the sea was very choppy and the little curach bounced along the wave-crests. Each time the boat crested a swell and then nosed into a trough, Aífe was misted with salty sea-spray, but she was well protected by boiled wool mittens, a cowled cape, and thick socks. The wool had been lightly soaked in oil, a fisherman's trick to ward off the sea. Ruadh had bartered for these when he got the boat from a fishing family.

She had a wooden cup for bailing and an oiled leather tarp in case of a squall. She carefully rationed her little leather bag of water and her store of oat bread and cheese. As the sun set, she surrendered to yet another bout of tears; there was no one to hear her except the fish and the birds.

"What do you want of me?" she called to the gods as she pounded her thigh. "Why me? I am no great poet or prophet, with a 'tongue that cannot lie'—I am just me! Just me, with everything that I love taken away." Aífe sobbed and hugged herself, feeling the emptiness spreading around her, feeling her small self in the middle of a vast, terrifying nothing. Her only comfort left was the stone that Gaine had given her when she was in the *nemed*. She clutched it in her tear-stained fingers and curled into the bottom of the boat as best she could, crying herself to sleep, rocked by the rhythm of the waves.

She woke at dawn to watch the red-orange orb of the sun melt gradually into gold and then yellow against a bluer and bluer sky.

"Grian, help me!" she called out to the rising Queen of the Day. She sat for hour upon hour, surrounded by only the sea and sky. No birds dipped from the wind, no fish broke the water's surface. Her back and shoulders ached, the sun beat down, and the waves pulled inexorably at the boat.

Then, without warning, the ocean flattened into glassy calm. The wind stopped. Sound didn't exist. Aífe looked all around her. There was nothing. She pulled into herself and scanned the waters again. In the far distance was a fast-approaching chariot with horse and rider, coursing towards her atop the glassy-still sea.

She dared not move, unsure whether this was a dream, a waking dream, or a vision. She squeezed her eyes once and opened them again to see if this was a fear-induced hallucination, a trick of the light. But the image persisted and grew larger. There was no mistaking it.

As the chariot drew nearer, the sea sprouted purple flowers, as if the boat were resting on a heather-filled moor. But Aífe was too terrified to touch the flowers. Then a shimmering silver mist rose on every side, blotting out the horizon.

The chariot and rider pulled up before her; it was a man with dark, flowing hair and beard and eyes the color of a winter's sky. The prancing horse was tall and proud, with a thick mane and tail so long it swept the field of flowers.

As the man studied her face, his billowing cloak changed colors as if registering his thoughts. It shimmered blue-green as a clear lake on a summer day; then silvered as moonlight. It darkened purple and then blackened as twilight. An intricately crafted sword hung by his side, glowing with its own light.

"I am the gatekeeper of Innis nan Druidneach. No one may approach except through me," he said. "What is it that you want?"

"I don't know!" Aífe cried. What was she supposed to say? What was she supposed to do?

"What is your purpose?" the man pointedly asked.

"I have been sent to learn." It was all she could think to say. She didn't know whether she should look directly at the rider or look away; she didn't know which would show respect. She was overwhelmed and shaken beyond her depth. There had been no time to prepare.

"That answer is good. I have heard worse. This is the place of all knowledge." He reached to the floor of the chariot, lifted up a small harp, and began to play. As he struck the first chord, Aífe's fear melted. The man spoke gently to the accompaniment of his harp.

"To obtain wisdom, you must drink from the Well of Five Streams. The well is eternal and inexhaustible. The well exists under the sea and also within you; you have carried it with you through birth and death, through countless lifetimes.

"The five streams are your senses. You must drink from the streams and from the well itself. Only then will you attain all knowledge. Remember my words. You must drink from the spiritual source and also from your own experience. Do you understand?"

"I think I do," she answered.

"You are young in this life. It will become clearer after you have finished your training."

"How did you know?" she asked, amazed that the stranger had divined the purpose of her journey.

"I will open the veil for you. You have a good heart, and you may pass."

He said nothing more.

As the silver mists parted, Aífe was surprised to see a small, rocky island in the distance. The chariot was turning; the man was leaving, heading back to the open ocean.

"Who are you?" she cried out as the choppy waves and winds reappeared in full force.

"Manannán mac Lir!" he shouted, his voice and form, chariot and horse already fading into the waves and the sea winds.

part two

The Druid Isle

28

S tunned by the encounter with the God of the Sea, Aífe sat frozen as the tiny craft nosed inexorably towards land, seemingly with a mind of its own. She saw a huge rock directly ahead, jutting out of the swelling surf just before the shoreline.

"Gods, please don't let me crash into that rock!" she prayed.

With no oars, she was helpless; the wind and waves would take her wherever they willed.

In the distance, she could make out a lone figure with long white hair standing on the beach. He appeared to be dressed in a knee-length blue robe.

As the curach drew closer to the rock, she wondered if she would have to jump and tried to quickly decide what to take with her if she did. She was just removing the wool cloak when the boat was sucked into a whirlpool spiraling around the huge stone. Too late! If she jumped now, she would be dragged under. She clutched the sides of the curach in terror.

"Help me!" she said to whatever force or being might be listening.

The boat was captured in the tiny maelstrom and swirled *dessel* around the rock, then spun out of the spiraling waters just as quickly into the frothing surf, arrowing straight for shore.

Curiously, the figure in blue made no offer of assistance. He just stood there, leaning on a carved staff, watching.

The curach rode a last wave onto the pebbled beach and came to a grinding stop right at the feet of the waiting man. Aífe could see that he was a Drui; his head was shaved from ear to ear in the Druid tonsure, and he wore a golden torc, which further advertised his status. The man's face was lined by age yet strangely youthful. Good will and humor radiated from him in waves, but he still hadn't moved to help her.

"The gods be with you, and welcome to Innis nan Druidneach," he said. "I am Amalgáid." He finally reached out his hand to help her step out of the curach. "I was waiting to see from which side of the rock you would arrive. It is lucky you came to shore *dessel*. The gods have accepted you and approve of your coming."

"What would have happened if I had come in the other way, *tuathamail?*" she asked, bewildered.

"We would have welcomed you just the same but sent you back after a few days' rest and a meal. May I offer you a Cup of Joy? It is our custom to welcome visitors with a drink of hospitality."

He reached into a large willow basket that was next to him on the pebbled beach and lifted out a corked stone bottle and a small golden cup. He opened the bottle, poured a thin stream of golden liquid into the cup, and presented it to her formally. "Welcome to the island," he said as she sipped the intoxicating cup of *mid*.

The man was relaxed, friendly, and not at all surprised by her arrival. Apparently this was not the first time a stranger had appeared from the ocean without any oars.

"You will go to the women's house, where you will be given your own room. After a few days' rest, your training will start," he said.

"You're not surprised to see me; how did you know I was coming?" she asked, mystified.

"We get one initiate about this time every year. The elders of Ériu always select one dedicant to place into the waves, and this year it was you. It is my job to stand on the beach and keep watch during the day. Bébinn watches by night. Now that you have arrived, we can all relax, and you can see to your studies," he said with an easy smile.

Amalgáid was one of the senior Druid of Innis nan Druidneach. Like the other Druid, he had arrived on its shore from the island of Ériu, just as Aífe had, in a tiny curach with no oars. After his training, he returned to Ériu but was later sent back by the elders to supervise the teaching of male initiates. Bébinn's story was much the same, only the elders had placed her in charge of the female initiates.

Aífe marveled at Amalgáid's simple speech and manner, as if her strange journey were the most natural thing in the world. She thought of Gaine, Ruadh, and Ethne and of how worried they would be.

"I have loved ones; is there any way to let them know I have arrived safely?" she asked.

"Alas, no, there isn't. But they knew it was the will of the gods to get you here or not, and that it was also the will of the gods which way you would come around that rock. None of us can predict who will be accepted from year to year. One day, you too will have to choose which of your students makes the journey—a painful choice but necessary for our ways to continue in the world. For now, you have successfully passed the first test."

"What test?" Aífe was baffled; she had done nothing but try to survive and hold on to her life and her wits.

"You could have refused the journey. You could have given in to fear, jumped into the sea, and swum back to shore, as some do. The fact that you are here at all means that you had enough faith, courage, and determination to face death and the unknown. That is the first requisite for being a true ban-fili. Congratulations." He bowed his head slightly in her direction, showing respect for her accomplishment.

Aífe realized that when Ethne had made the decision to leave the nemed and live in the forest with no hope of further support, she too had faced the challenge of the unknown and won. Ruadh had also undergone his own private initiation each time he offered his life to protect others. Suddenly she was aware of the intense sacrifices that had been made to benefit other lives, including her own. She pondered the enormity of this as they walked up the pebble-strewn beach, onto the sand dunes, and along the eastern shore.

As they walked, she saw that the island was densely covered in yew, with pockets of oak, ash, and elm in the sunnier spots. Her herbalist's eye catalogued the healing worts along the way: plantain and terrestrial sun among the grasses; heather in the bogs; birch, willow, and alder by the streams.

"It must be very difficult to farm in a place like this," she commented.

"Oh, we don't farm. We depend upon wild animals such as gulls, geese, seals, and fish, and we get gifts of grain from the mainland from time to time. We collect seaweeds for food and the seeds and shoots of wild edibles that we plant inside the earthen bank that surrounds our settlement. The bank protects the tender plants from the sea winds.

"We have rowan, elder, hawthorn, and crabapple trees for food and medicine, and just enough wildflowers to keep the bees happy."

Aífe saw that their way of existence was even simpler than the life she had known at the Forest School. It was all very humble, yet the man seemed healthy, happy, and well dressed.

At length, they reached the earthen bank and entered the tiny settlement through a gap in the earthen wall. A small crowd of Druid emerged from round stone houses to greet them, and a tall, thin woman with long red hair and sparkling eyes the color of robin's eggs stretched out her hand in formal greeting. Her face, like Amalgáid's, was youthful yet lined with age, lines that bespoke a quiet joy.

"I am Bébinn. Welcome to our *tuath*," she said with a smile.

Another woman, shorter and blond, with warm chestnut-brown eyes, stepped forward to introduce herself as well. "I am Dáiríne; I will help you with anything you need in the way of clothing or other supplies."

Dáiríne was one of the Druid who performed tasks to aid others. Everyone on Innis nan Druidneach was a full initiate, and they were each assigned occupations that suited their nature. Some tended plants and trees; others kept bees or wove and sewed cloth. Some set snares for animals and fish; others chopped wood, fetched water, or cooked and kept house. Others were teachers.

There was no hierarchy in these tasks; everyone was an equally valued member of the community, ready to give spiritual counseling and advice to dedicants and laypeople alike.

Aífe's stomach suddenly growled so loudly that everyone could hear.

"We are preparing a small feast in your honor," Dáiríne quickly said, grinning.

The entire community escorted Aífe to the large central roundhouse, reserved for mixed functions of both women and men. A fire blazed in the central hearth, and the smell of cooking made Aífe feel suddenly weak. As they waited for the food to appear, she was peppered with questions about who she was, where she had come from, and any news of Ériu she might bring.

In particular, they wanted to hear every detail of her trip over the ocean in the tiny craft. She fought embarrassment and finally revealed her encounter with the man who called himself Manannán and the *féth* that surrounded the curach when she met him. She was afraid they would think she was insane, but the effect was just the opposite. To her amazement, they were very favorably impressed.

After a meal of red-deer stew, oatmeal bannocks, and baked wild apples with hazelnuts and honey, she was shown to her bath and bed. She was assigned a private bedchamber in the women's house, which was partitioned into rooms by tall wooden screens of carved yew that spoked around the central hearth. Between each partition of the house there was a plump heather-filled mattress covered with linen sheets and woolen blankets.

Other amenities of her private sleeping enclosure were a brazier against the chill, a tall candlestick with one large beeswax candle, a carved chest for personal belongings, and a bronze pot for bodily needs. Two wooden bathtubs were positioned near the central fire, where a huge cauldron of water had already been set to simmer. She gratefully accepted the offer of a long, hot soak and a scrub with lavender-scented *siabainn*.

After Aífe had bathed long enough to remove all trace of chill from her bones, Dáiríne handed her two soft sleeping robes of lamb's wool, a woolen cape, and several tunics, each dyed green with heather tips, alder, and birch bark.

"These will be your uniform while you are here; all the women wear green and all the men wear blue, the colors of the earth and sky. Bébinn will fetch you in the morning."

Before retiring for the night, Aífe carefully laid the stone that Gaine had gifted her beside the candle and sat on her bed, meditating to ground and center her mind and body and to calm her nerves and spirit. Her hands lay relaxed, palms up, on her thighs, and her eyes were closed lightly.

Suddenly her Sight saw each of her palms filled with fire, as if she were holding balls of living flame. A third ball of white fire materialized before her. Within the white fire were mandalas and kaleidoscopes of color changing and interchanging until everything resolved into the simple form of a white lily. She found herself gazing into the center of the blazing white flower. In the exact center were an infant, then two, then three, until the three babies made a triangle. She heard a voice:

"This is who you are now. You are at the beginning of your journey to understand the nature of your mind, body, and spirit. Focus on all three. Bless them. Give them your full attention. Attention is love."

She shivered violently for a moment and then opened her eyes. *I have no idea who that was. I'll have to ask Bébinn in the morning,* she thought, pulling back the covers and stretching her legs onto the soft heather mattress, already drifting to sleep in the warm darkness of the bedchamber.

29

*Y*ou have a powerful connection to spirit: first Manannán himself
opened the way for you, and now you have been blessed with a
spirit guide," said Bébinn, happy because it presaged a good outcome
for Aífe's apprenticeship.

"I have my teachers to thank for that. Ethne and Ruadh shared
everything they knew with me at the Forest School, for which I am
very grateful," Aífe replied.

Bébinn approved of Aífe's humility and respect for her elders. She
would pass along the knowledge that the Forest School was an excellent institution of learning.

They spent the next few days exploring the length and breadth of
the island so that Aífe would be familiar with every part. It was a small
place; in just two days of leisurely walking, they had covered the entire
shoreline and all the important points inland. Aífe was struck by the
towering yews that dominated the landscape.

Bébinn explained, "The yews are one reason that the ancient ones
first came here. These trees have the ability to live forever. Before they
die, they send out shoots and grow their children around them in a
ring, ensuring that their line goes on and on. We try to emulate them.
In this way, our teachings have lasted for thousands of sun-cycles.

"There are sun-turnings when the yews go dormant; they will simply stop growing when conditions are unfavorable. There are other

times when they grow again in spurts. Growing a yew tree is a very slow process. When we receive a promising student such as you, it is as if the yews of Innis nan Druidneach have sent out the call that it is once again the time for a renewal of the growth cycle.

"In the morning after you break your fast, I want you to meet me at the south end of the island, on the pebble beach where you first landed. There we will begin your studies."

The next morning, they met at sunrise and sat on the pebbled beach, quietly watching the waves come in.

At last Bébinn broke the silence. "Your teachers told you that you were coming here to study *filidecht*, did they not? Most have a very poor understanding of what that means. The *fili*, as you know, must master storytelling and many different rhymes and meters. They have to be master or mistress of the art of composition. But what we teach here is something very different. We teach the *inner* content of poems, the eternal spiritual truth that the poems are designed to capture.

"It has been said that if our students understood beforehand the nature of this work, they wouldn't touch it with a barge pole. There is little glamour in these teachings, even if you were allowed admittance by a Sea God. One of your major tasks here will be to fight boredom. This is real work. Do you understand me?" Bébinn searched Aífe's face for any trace of indolence.

"I am not afraid of hard work. I look forward to the challenge!"

"Very well, then, we will start with *ecnae nathairech*, or serpent wisdom. Have you heard of it?"

"No, I haven't. I am familiar with *ecnae bratánech*, the salmon wisdom—but that must be something different."

"In a way, they are related," Bébinn replied. "You already know how to use your salmon wisdom to get to the source of an answer. When your serpent wisdom is activated, you will feel a heat and a tingling sensation up your spine. If properly activated, the serpent wisdom energizes all of your body centers. Part of the magic of this island is that it speeds up the process in a way that would be inconceivable anywhere else.

"There are two channels, one on either side of your spine, that cross and recross as the serpent energy twines upwards. Once this happens, you will be filled with unshakable confidence and true spiritual vision, and you will be kind to all creatures ever after. The raising of this energy is called 'riding the serpent within.'

"As you know, serpents are the guardians of treasure. The dragons that you have heard about in stories are actually flying serpents, which are said to hoard treasure and protect it for many centuries by sleeping on it in their cave. But for you the cave is your heart, a secret inner space that no one but you can see. You will have to go within the inner cave of your own heart to find your own special treasures."

"I always thought that serpents and dragons were fearsome things that could lay waste to the countryside and burn you to a crisp!" said Aífe.

"Yes, serpents have a poison in their mouth that can kill you if they bite. But you too have poisons in your mouth and in your mind. If you hold those poisons within and witness them without judgment, and learn to purify them using your serpent energy, they will turn from a deadly substance into a precious gem. That is what we will teach you how to do here on Innis nan Druidneach. We will take you far beyond the personality that you have developed at your Forest School, the self that has been fashioned by your life experiences so far. Our task is to teach you the path of your true self, the self you had before you were born. If we succeed, you will tap into this knowledge for the rest of your life and even into your next life and beyond."

"By going within, using my serpent wisdom?"

"Yes, exactly. Once attained, this knowledge will be accessible to you forever."

They were silent for a long while as Aífe digested the information. The only sounds were the cries of distant gulls and the gentle lapping of the surf on the small green, red, and white stones. Finally, Aífe broached a question.

"Why did you bring me to the south end of the island again?"

"I brought you here for a very specific reason. I mentioned earlier that the awakened serpent energy activates certain body centers. This island has centers of power—pools of energy—just as you have within your own body. We will study the energies of the landscape in some detail, and as you come to know the island, you will also come to know yourself. This island is a map that will help you to understand who you really are."

Aífe wasn't sure she followed Bébinn's train of thought, but she held her tongue, thinking it would make sense over time.

"The first step in your education was the test of your willingness to come here at all," Bébinn said.

"Yes, Amalgáid explained that to me earlier."

"That test is called the test of the black stone, or *cristall dub*, a type of dark smoky quartz that comes from the mountains of Caledonia. By passing that test, you activated and mastered a specific energy center, or *bríg*, in your body: the pool of energy that exists in your bowels. It is the place of the first and most basic instinct of life: raw survival. It governs the very ground of your being. It is your fear for self-preservation.

"Those who have not mastered this most primal emotion can be easily led to violence. This is the fear that lies at the root of all wars.

"When you made the choice to step into that coracle, you controlled and mastered the most basic fear of all living creatures: dissolution of the body. Whether you knew it or not, you grounded yourself in the strength and power of the deep earth and found the courage to continue. By persevering despite your fear, you learned the lesson of stability in the midst of chaos. The chaos was the open sea, and the successful outcome of your test was your safe arrival on the shore of Innis nan Druidneach.

"From now on, whenever you face a chaotic situation, you can recall the memory of this first test, and it will help you through it. And you can also use an actual *cristall dub* to help you. You can keep it in your crane bag and call on it any time you need its powers."

"My crane bag?" Aífe asked, puzzled.

"It's a power bundle into which you place your most important magical tools and treasures. No one can tell you what goes inside because it's your own personal magical amulet. A Drui may put herbs, stones, tree parts, or any other objects of power into his or her crane bag. Some like to add a piece of lightning-struck oak to energize it. The herb dragon's blood works that way too."

"But why is it called a crane bag?"

"The crane is a creature that exists in three worlds simultaneously. It has its feet in the water, which corresponds to the *Sidhe* realm of the ancestors; its body is on the earth, just like any other creature; and it can fly through the sky realm. It is a living symbol of Druid magic and the ability to move between the worlds of land, sea, and sky, of the ancestors, the nature spirits, and the gods.

"A crane steps very deliberately as it walks, first picking up one foot and carefully putting it down before picking up the other. Druids too must act with focused care when attempting to alter the web of the world. And the crane is a bird that calls out to other birds when it senses danger. It acts on behalf of all creatures, not just for itself and its own family."

"I think I see now," Aífe said.

Bébinn went on. "You can hold the *cristall dub* in your hand or put it into your crane bag and carry it with you, or simply call on its powers in your mind whenever you are under the influence of confusion, glamour, or intoxication. It will give you grounding and stability and help you to pull things together in your mind and your spirit.

"You can also place it over the bowels of a person who needs healing in that part of their body. It will stir up energy, if that is what is called for, or stabilize energy, if that is what is needed. It is a very intelligent stone when used by a competent healer, which I know you are."

Bébinn reached into a fold of her tunic and pulled out a small leather bag. She searched inside for a moment and drew out a small object. "This is for you," she said, handing the object to Aífe. It was a clear brown *cristall dub*.

"Hold the stone and get to know it. Become familiar with its energy. You can place it under your pillow tonight and allow it to settle into your dreams. Later you can store it in your crane bag." She pressed the empty leather bag into Aífe's palm. Aífe was already planning to keep Gaine's stone with the dark crystal, because it had helped her withstand the test of the sea.

"Now it's time to walk back for the afternoon meal. I heard that Dáiríne is making her famous mushroom pies."

30

The next day, they walked to a sandy cove on the western side of the island, facing the open sea. The cove was part of a long and wide horseshoe-shaped beach called the Bay at the Back of the Ocean. In contrast to the pebbly shore of the south end of the island, the western beach was covered in fine, powdery sand.

Bébinn had brought a blue woolen blanket and a basket of provisions. She spread the blanket on the soft sand and laid out an assortment of beautifully cut fruits, shelled nuts, spirals of cheese, oat cakes, and fragrant honey-wine in a lovely silver cup.

"What do you feel as we sit here on this soft woolen blanket surrounded by all of this food?" Bébinn asked.

"I feel surrounded by comfort and beauty—the beauty of the bay, the warm sands, and the carefully prepared foods. The white birds flying above us feed my spirit and nourish my heart. I feel that all my senses are comforted at once. I could not wish for anything more."

"Exactly. We came here today to experience pleasure: beauty, harmony, and the fulfillment of desire. Go ahead, enjoy yourself—eat anything you want, and have some wine too."

Aífe ate until she had had enough and then stretched out on the blanket, basking in the sunshine, perfectly content.

"I want you to continue eating," Bébinn said.

"But I'm not hungry anymore," Aífe murmured, too content to move.

"Nevertheless, I want you to finish the entire bottle of honey-wine and eat all the remaining food. I am going for a short walk, and when I come back, I want it to be gone from sight."

The pleasant morning had turned into something else.

Aífe did as she was told and soon felt terrible. She had an upset stomach and a massive headache as she waited in misery for Bébinn to return. At last, Bébinn reappeared. She had filled the empty food basket with fresh mussels and packed them in cold, wet seaweed to take them back to the Main House. The sight and scent of the mussels made Aífe dizzy.

"How are you feeling?" Bébinn asked innocently.

"I think I am going to be sick," Aífe replied. She stood up and ran behind a nearby rock, where she vomited up everything she had just eaten. When she returned, Bébinn patiently continued her instruction as if nothing untoward had happened.

"Today's lesson is about desire and how to handle it properly. When we feel a desire for a something—a person, an object, a place—we have to ask ourselves if the object of desire is truly helpful to us or if it is just a mindless craving. Sometimes we have emotional cravings that lead to compulsions, and these can harm the beauty and balance of our life. Addictions to food, music, beautiful clothes and jewelry, alcohol to excess, cravings for sexual pleasure and other mindless habits can ruin friendships and destroy lives.

"On this path we do not deny ourselves pleasure. If we have a strong desire for something, we experience it completely, and then we learn the consequences of fulfilling that desire. If the result does not bring balance, vigor, confidence, beauty, harmony, and happy relationships into our life, then we let it go, whatever it is. We enjoy all the things that life has to offer, but we strive for balance and moderation in all things.

"The seat of desire is pooled three fingers below your navel, here…"

She showed Aífe how to find that particular spot, using her hand to demonstrate.

"We have to learn the difference between healthy fulfillment of our hopes and dreams and compulsive cravings. Now that you have had this experience with food and drink, you will be able to recall the lesson whenever your blind desire threatens to take control. This lesson is called *mían*, or the test of desire."

Bébinn reached into her pouch and pulled out a clear, polished amber nugget, a stone the color of liquid sunlight. "This is for you—a gift to remember this day."

"How could I ever forget it?" Aífe said with a rueful laugh. "Amber is a stone I am very familiar with. The women of Ériu often wear it as a talisman of protection and as a symbol of rank. Ethne, my teacher, has a large piece that she carries with her when she attends a woman in labor. She has the mother-to-be hold it in her hand. She says it helps cut the labor pains."

Bébinn explained, "Amber is protective and soothing because it's a perfect balance of fire and water. It brings peace and harmony to turbulent emotions, and it, along with all orange stones, has an affinity for the female and male reproductive organs. You can place an orange stone like amber over the spleen or reproductive organs to heal and balance them.

"If we use such a stone in our spiritual practice, it will enable us to channel our creative and sexual energies to spiritual development. It can also help us transform our desire for material objects and substances into a desire for a harmonious life filled with beauty.

"Are you feeling better now?" Bébinn asked.

"Yes, thank you, I am."

Aífe fingered the amber nugget all the way back to the Druid settlement; her stomach and senses were soothed by its smooth, honey-colored form.

31

The next day they walked to a rocky outcrop at the back of the western beach, known as the Eagle's Beak.

"How is your stomach feeling today?" Bébinn asked, knowing that Aífe had not eaten since the day before.

"I'm fine, thanks, as long as I drink only water," Aífe said good-naturedly.

"Do you see that rocky prominence up there? I want you to climb it."

Aífe looked up, horrified. It appeared to be a sheer cliff from where they were standing.

"If you go slowly, you will find little handholds and places to put your feet. It isn't as hard as it looks."

"I have never climbed anything like that! What if I fall?" Aífe clenched her hands.

"Don't ask questions or give excuses. Do it now!"

Aífe had never attempted such a thing in her life. It was a good forty feet to the top of the rocks, and she was terrified that she would fall and smash her skull on the rocks below. The first ten feet were easy, the next few harder. By the time she was halfway up, the height was dizzying, and she was too afraid to look down.

Each time her foot slipped off of a rocky purchase her stomach lurched, until she was covered in sweat. She uttered small gasps each time she lost her footing. She thought of the soft sand between the rocks below. If she fell, would it cushion her? Might she only break a few bones?

Near the top, her progress was by inches. Now she felt like a fly clinging to a sheer wall, about to be swiped off by some giant, unseen hand at any moment. She used every bit of willpower just to keep going, despite her trembling limbs. When at last she pulled herself over the top and flopped onto a small tussock of grass at the summit, she was stunned to see Bébinn there before her, calmly sitting on a fleecy blanket, laying out provisions for a picnic.

"But how ... ?" was all she could say between pants of exhaustion and slowly ebbing fear.

"There's a grassy slope up the back. It's an easy climb. I got here before you were even halfway up the rocks!" said Bébinn, smiling innocently.

Aífe grew angry. She had been tricked and deceived but dared not show it. It was impolite to hold such ill feeling towards an elder.

Bébinn studied her face for a moment.

"Tell me how you feel. Be honest!"

"I'm hurt, and I'm angry. Why did you do that to me? I could have been killed!"

"I suppose that's true. Why then did you do it?"

"Because you said I had to!"

"As I recall, I said I wanted you to climb. Just because I wanted you to climb up that rock, did that mean you had to? Did you have a choice?" Bébinn inquired calmly.

"I didn't think I had a choice," Aífe answered.

"You chose not to have a choice. But you were never a victim. You made your own decision. Your choice was to follow my dictate. Yes?"

"I suppose that's true." Aífe was still confused.

"I do not have power over you. You made the decision to go up that rock face and not seek another path."

Aífe stood quietly and thought. "Yes," she finally answered. "I decided." She was amazed and embarrassed. Through all the fear and discomfort, she had been angry at following someone else's orders. Now she saw that she had been in control of her own fate all along; she had simply made the wrong choice.

Bébinn continued. "Today's lesson is called *commus*. It is about power and the choices we make to use or not use our own power. We will focus on the area around your stomach, between your navel and the bottom of your rib cage." Bébinn indicated the space with her fingers and went on speaking. "When a woman is pregnant, the fetus develops in the center of the mother's body. There is a reason for that. The growth of a child is a physical and visible manifestation of the transformational power that exists in the middle of the body. But there are other powers and energies that also emanate from that same area. The center of the body is the place from which all of the body's powers radiate.

"On a base level, the nature of that area has to do with developing power over others or letting others have power over us. You see, there is a constant tension in our lives between the quest for personal empowerment and making positive choices versus exerting power over others or being overpowered by others.

"Sometimes we do need to assert ourselves powerfully, but if this becomes a habitual pattern of life, it results in harm to ourselves and others. It can even make us physically sick and create chronic stomach disease. Of course, constantly feeling victimized and powerless can lead to disease just as easily.

"It is especially important when we do magic that we remember that all magic comes back to the sender eventually. If we seek magical power over someone else, it will eventually backfire—and the same energy will return to harm *us* three times."

Aife was thoughtful. "Yes, Ethne always says that a wise magician has to remember that the universe tends towards balance. If forceful energy is sent out—for example, battle-magic—it will rebound on the sender. The old Ard-Drui Coemgen died doing battle-magic for the Ard-Ri Crimthann."

"Exactly. Nature is the ultimate source of all power, and she always seeks to bring the world into balance. All beings must be respected because they, we, are all part of Great Nature. We are all part of the same Source and equally sacred. We should strive for respect and cooperation in all things to get what we want, rather than trying to exert power over others.

"There are many kinds of power: power over, passive power, self-empowerment, and true personal power. Sometimes a person will even play the victim as a way to gain power over others. We always have a choice in our use of power: action or inaction, speaking or not speaking, doing or not doing.

"The center of our body, the place from which our power emanates or where power is taken in, is also the place of transition between the pools of energy in our body above and the pools of energy below. It is the choice-point where we decide whether to move forward and change or persevere with who we already are.

"This constant decision-making produces a friction within us that vitalizes all our bodily energies, just as the sun energizes the plants. It leads to change and transformation, if honored, while if ignored, keeps us stuck in our habitual patterns. It can arouse a lust for life and new challenges or make us feel weak and helpless. We have to consciously decide whether to move forward, change, and transform, or remain the same.

"But the key is to realize that we are always choosing to use our power or choosing not to use it. No doubt your Ard-Drui Coemgen was well aware of the risks when he undertook battle-magic on behalf of the Ard-Ri. He made a conscious decision to sacrifice himself for the good of other lives, as a great Drui sometimes will."

They were silent for a moment, each reflecting on the Druid who had given their lives throughout the ages so that their tribes would prosper. They had volunteered to be sacrificed and shed their life-blood to return their energies to the land, to ensure healthy crops for the people, or to protect the tribes from disease, conquest, or some other looming catastrophe.

"Why did we come here, to the Eagle's Beak?" Aífe asked at last.

Bébinn replied, "You know the story of the King of the Birds. In that tale, which is actually a wisdom teaching, there was a contest amongst the birds of the world. The challenge was that whichever bird flew highest would win the title King of the Birds. One by one, the birds stepped up to claim the prize.

"The snow goose was sure she would win because she migrated vast distances each spring and fall. The raven was full of magic and believed she would win by virtue of her cunning. The eagle was sure he would win because he had the strongest wings.

"On the day of the contest, the birds flew higher and higher until finally the lordly eagle flew above all the rest, circling easily in the clouds. But when even he could climb no higher, a tiny wren appeared from within the eagle's back feathers. The wren had hidden himself in the eagle's feathers before the eagle took off, without the eagle even knowing it. The wren flew higher than the mighty eagle because he was well rested, and in that way the wren was proclaimed the King of the Birds.

"The wren is known as the 'Druid bird' because it symbolizes using one's brains rather than brawn to achieve one's aims. The eagle is a symbol of using raw muscle to achieve power, which is a long way of explaining why we came to this spot. If we want to maintain our personal power, it is a good idea to think carefully before we act and not rely on brute physical force, as the eagle did."

"Oh," said Aífe quietly. She now saw how she had charged ahead without thinking and used her muscles and will to climb the cliff, instead of using her mind to see if there was another, better way.

Bébinn spoke again as she finished laying out the midday meal. "Today's test is called the test of citrine. Citrine is a stone of fire and the sun. It is used to heal the digestive tract by laying it over the stomach, and it reminds us that we should make positive use of our personal power in the pursuit of our goals. It also reminds us that just as too much sunlight will burn us and too little will cause the crops to fail, so too much exertion of power or too little exertion of it will bring a lack of balance and cause harm."

Bébinn reached into her willow basket and pulled out a folded linen cloth, which she opened carefully. In the center was a shiny citrine crystal, sparkling orange in the sunlight. She handed it to Aífe.

"This is for your crane bag. Now, let's sit on top of the Eagle's Beak and pretend we are both tiny wrens. Dáiríne packed a nice lunch for us, and I think your belly is probably settled enough to enjoy it!"

"Thank you very much!" Aífe murmured gratefully. Her stomach had indeed recovered from the trials of the day before, and she found that she was suddenly starving.

32

When they got back to the Main House in the evening, the place was in an uproar.

"This has never happened—never in the whole history of Innis nan Druidneach!" Dáiríne declared.

The Druid declaimed and recalled out loud the history of the island. None of them had ever heard of such a thing.

"It is the will of the gods! He came right around the rock *dessel*—I saw it myself!" said Amalgáid. He had been searching for sphagnum moss in the forest for the dressing of wounds when he spied the tiny curach spinning *dessel* around the great rock at the south end.

"I dropped my basket of moss on the trail because I was so surprised!" he added.

"Where is he now? Has he been welcomed properly?" Dáiríne asked.

"I left him outside the earthen bank. I did not want to let him in until I heard everyone's decision," Amalgáid said.

"Poor thing, he must be wet and very cold. Bring him in. We'll ask him how he got here," said Báetán, the Drui who most often took care of the bees.

It was said that Báetán could speak to bees and understand their language. Sometimes he was seen dancing with the bees on sunny days.

"Those are honeyed words from you, Báetán," said Amalgáid. "Let's hear what the young man has to say."

They ushered the stranger into the Main House. He was wet, cold, hungry, and resembled a lost water creature foundering on dry land.

"How did you come to be out at sea all by yourself in that ridiculously small boat?" Amalgáid asked, opening the inquiry.

Dáiríne was already swinging an iron cauldron over the central hearth to prepare a posset of elderberries, honey, and the Waters of Life to stave off a chill. Báetán ran to the men's house to fetch warm clothing for the stranger.

"My boat is not ridiculous," the stranger said, standing straighter for emphasis.

"Where do you come from, and who are your people?" Bébinn asked.

"I am Lucius, a Galli from Inissi Leuca," he said.

Their faces went blank. No one recognized the place.

"I was raised there as a *Cristaide*, but I seem to have left that way of life. I no longer know exactly what religion I am … and now I am here."

"Who brought you here?" Amalgáid asked, concerned that the sanctity of the Druid Isle had been breached, and wondering why and how a *Cristaide* could have possibly been admitted into their sacred space.

"No one brought me here. I left Inissi Leuca in that curach, and it has borne me safely across the open seas."

"You came all the way from Gallia in that curach?" asked Amalgáid, aghast. In all his sun-seasons of living, he had never heard of such seamanship.

"I had some help. I escaped the Romani so that I wouldn't be taken as a slave, then I was blown by a tempest to Cornubia, where I met the tribe of Mamm an Bys. They fed me, gave me clothing, and treated me very well. But I decided to continue on, and with the help of the wind and the currents, I finally washed up on your beach." Lucius looked Amalgáid directly in the eye, as if defying him to contradict his story.

"What in the name of all the gods made you think you could travel the seas in a tiny boat like that?" asked Bébinn, who was having a hard time keeping her mouth from hanging open in wonder.

He looked around the room and suddenly realized that he was in the presence of holy people. He saw the men's tonsures, cut from ear to ear across the brow instead of in the circle at the top of their heads, and their simple but elegant robes, all of the same color, either blue or green. He thought maybe they were a hidden community of Druid, so he decided to risk the truth.

"Mamm an Bys came to me and told me I was protected. I trusted her." He looked slowly from one of them to the next.

They grew quiet and appraised the unexpected visitor. If his arrival was a surprise, his words were stunning.

Báetán had returned with the warm clothing and stood in the back, quietly listening. Aífe was listening too. She understood very well the ordeal of the open sea, and she felt his vulnerability. She also sensed sadness in him, as if he had lost something precious and was on a quest to find it. She quietly took the blue tunic, cape, and woolen socks from Báetán and shyly approached the stranger.

"Put these on. We don't want you to get sick." And when she raised her face and gazed into his eyes, she fell into a blue world of peace from which she never wanted to escape.

He in turn looked into her green eyes and tumbled down a verdant hill in springtime. Embarrassed, confused, excited, he tore his gaze away and waited for the crowd to decide his fate.

Amalgáid solemnly laid a hand on the stranger's shoulder.

"Who is Mamm an Bys?" he asked gently, as a test of the youth's sincerity.

"She is the Soul of the Earth. She is the Primal Mother from whom all things have sprung. She is as deep as the ocean and as high as the tallest mountain. She is the noblest tree in the forest and the sacred Source of every river." He hung his head. How could he possibly put her into mere words?

The Druid were convinced.

"It is the will of the gods," said Bébinn quietly. "For the first time in all the sun-cycles of this island, we have *two* initiates this summer."

Everyone nodded in agreement and wonder.

And so it was. The next day, Aífe continued her tests and initiations as the stranger named Lucius began his own training under the tutelage of the senior Drui, Amalgáid.

33

Lucius was given his own private enclosure in the men's house and outfitted with the blue garments that would mark him as a student of the island. Used to a communal life with monks and brothers, it all felt very natural, except for the presence of the women.

One morning Amalgáid led him to a grassy clearing in the forest, a little green glade filled with sunlight, where the ever-present wind and the sounds of the sea were at last stilled, absorbed by a thick ring of hazel and yew. A tiny brook looped its way in and out of grasses and leaves, then disappeared into pools and under rocks as it meandered its way softly towards the sea. Butterflies and honeybees ranged the lip of the little stream, seeking a sip of water, and everywhere colorful flowers opened their faces to the sun. The scent of the wildflowers and grasses rose in the moist, sunny air like a song, a palpable hum of vibrating color and light.

"This place is beautiful," said Lucius in a whisper, sensing a strong and mysterious presence there that he did not wish to disturb.

"This is where the mother deer come to give birth," said Amalgáid in a hushed tone. "Every year they come here because of the soft grasses, water, and peaceful silence. It has everything a deer mother could want for her newborn fawn."

They sat side by side in silent appreciation for a while, just soaking in the warm sunlight and the atmosphere. Slowly, one by one, mother deer and their fawns began emerging from the dark of the forest, stepping into the sunlight without fear. When the deer were sure that all was well, the does lowered their heads and began to graze while the fawns sported about, lunging at one another with tiny hooves and leaping into the air in mock fright.

"The joy you feel here is what comes of having a peaceful place to retire to," Amalgáid said. "A place like this bestows the freedom to eat, sleep, and play in contentment. It holds a sacred beauty that radiates to all creatures that come into it and heals the spirits of those who experience it. Everyone needs such a place for retreat, if not in a physical space, then in the temple of the mind. Have you such a sanctuary within you?"

"No, I haven't."

The idea of a mental sanctuary was novel. The only such places he had known were the churches of Gallia and perhaps the *fogo* of the tribe of Mamm an Bys.

"It is very important that you have an inner sanctuary to carry with you, a place within that you can enter when you need comfort. Thoughts are things, meaning that as you think, so your material reality will follow. You can visualize another in your inner sanctuary, should they need healing. You can visualize yourself or any other being in your inner sanctuary as healthy and whole in mind, spirit, and body. Your inner sanctuary holds infinite compassion for all beings in need.

"Today's lesson is called *cride*. It's about the heart, peace, compassion, and a serene relationship between yourself and all creatures. The center of the chest is the home of the heart, the seat of love. It is not the seat of pity or feeling sorry for others; that kind of feeling is born of feeling superior to others. The love that I speak of is also not romantic love; that kind of love always seeks something in return.

"The love I am describing is pure compassion, which breaks down the barriers between self and other and is the destroyer of duality. True compassion produces an impulse to help other lives simply because the act of helping others makes one happy. It is an automatic impulse, a way of life, a condition of forgiveness and of celebrating others' joys.

If someone has something that you lack, rather than feeling loss or regret, there is an automatic wish to celebrate the other person's good fortune.

"We have come to this place to experience the love that is inherent in Great Nature. She always seeks to support all creatures, if we but have the eyes to see it. We who live here easily survive on the bounty of our little island: the plants, trees, seaweeds, fish, and other creatures provide our food and medicine, and the stones and trees provide our homes and our fires. We trade for luxuries, but that is a choice we make. Nature is our Great Mother who unconditionally accepts all of her children and provides exactly what each one needs. We are always surrounded by her love, if we but have the eyes to see it and the heart to feel it."

"Is the sacred presence stronger in this spot? I find that I want to speak in whispers out of respect," Lucius asked.

"What you are experiencing is a direct connection to the Self, the eternal spirit or divine essence that dwells within all things. Some have given it the name of a goddess; they call her Nemetona. She is the invisible spirit that dwells within the sacred grove.

"To learn the true lesson of the heart, you must learn to hear the voice of Nemetona speaking to you from within the silence. Her voice, the voice of the spirit, is more important than anything we have learned from our parents, our teachers, or from society. When we are guided by that inner voice, it brings a purity of intention towards others that removes all doubt, worry, and fear. We feel secure and confident, and good fortune, love, and healthy relationships follow as naturally as the sun that shines upon the flowers."

Lucius took in the words but found his mind straying towards the beautiful young woman who at that very moment was making her own progress through the lessons of the island. He hardly dared admit it, but he was already bound by her gaze. He hoped he would find a way to get to know her better, and maybe bring her to this beautiful place alone one sunny day.

And he was surprised to find that he was already letting go of the memory of Aurelia. It seemed a miracle that he had found himself drawn to two fascinating women in such a short time—a strange fate for one who had so recently left the brothers of Inissi Leuca.

"Your mind is drifting away, Lucius. You are in a world of your own," Amalgáid said with a wry smile. Lucius blushed; it was as if the man had read his thoughts.

"Here, I have a gift for your crane bag." Amalgáid took a polished stone heart of *cristall grisainech* from his pocket and pressed it into Lucius's hand.

The island suddenly spoke to Lucius through the stone. He felt and heard its living, breathing being. And somewhere in the middle of this unspoken conversation, there were images of the green-eyed young woman he had recently met. This "lesson of the heart" could be no coincidence.

"Put the stone over a person's heart to heal it, and it will help mend sorrow and loss as well as physical heart pain. The heart is the balance point between the basic survival needs of the lower body and the spiritual realms that correspond to pools of energy in the upper body. That stone will help you and others to move their consciousness from the worldly to the spiritual."

As Amalgáid spoke, an inquisitive fawn edged closer, snuffling the air with curiosity. Lucius stared into its liquid brown eyes. He had never seen a creature so delicate or beautiful.

"Carry the memory of this place in your heart forever, Lucius. Come back to it in your mind when you need a sanctuary from life's sharp edges," Amalgáid said, reaching into his willow basket for apples.

As they fed the deer from their hands, Lucius thought of Ísu distributing loaves and fishes to the multitude. *How strange. Suddenly the apples and the deer are as sacred to me as the body of Ísu ever was. The trees, the stones, the deer, and the Druid of this island are sacred, as are Aífe and I. We are all wrapped in the divine; it is everywhere, within and without us, in an endless mystery.*

34

That night Aífe approached Lucius as she carried a pitcher of *mid* around the main hall, refilling cups. Lucius's cup was still full as he sat wrapped in thought next to the fire. His mind was too wholly taken up with the day's events to pay much attention to food and drink.

Aífe paused as she came nearer, put the pitcher down, and sat down next to him. They were both facing the hearth.

"Did it go well for you today?" she asked.

Lucius turned to her, his eyes not quite focused on his surroundings.

"Did it go well?" she repeated.

He blinked and found himself staring once more into the eyes that had nearly swamped him. "Go well?"

"Yes, did you like your lessons?"

He grinned. "*Like* isn't exactly the word I would use, but, yes, the lessons made new places inside me."

"Ah!" Aífe gave a little clap. "Yes! That's it exactly!"

Before either could say another word, Bébinn and Amalgáid were beside them.

"This is not permitted," Bébinn said. "You may not share stories or thoughts of your lessons. Each lesson is crafted for the individual student!"

"That is correct," said Amalgáid. "You each have but a short time to be here, and you must not be distracted. It is your job and your duty to take in all that we offer and carry it back out to the world. Thus it has ever been for the dedicants who come to us."

Bébinn led Aífe away, and Amalgáid stood so as to block Lucius's view of the young woman. He knew what a distraction a youthful member of the opposite sex could be. But why, between earth and the heavens, had the gods chosen two of them? It was a mystery. Training both of them at the same time was already proving difficult.

After that, Lucius and Aífe were careful not to speak to or come near one another, but they still could not avoid each other's eyes.

The next morning, Bébinn addressed Aífe while they were in the women's quarters before the morning meal. "You must prepare to spend some nights in the wild. We will remain outside however long it takes until you accomplish your task."

"Where are we going this time?" Aífe's curiosity mingled with trepidation.

"To the cliffs of the western shore, where you will learn the lesson called *fúaimm*," Bébinn replied.

They packed extra bedding and rolled it into oiled leather tarps, which they tied with ropes to sling onto their backs. Aífe took out the oiled wool clothing she had worn on her passage across the sea in case of inclement weather and dressed in layers for the journey. Each packed a large basket of bread, water, apples, and cheese and cut several stout poles for a lean-to.

The day was warm, and by the time they had crossed the island and reached the western beach, they were drenched with perspiration.

"The sunlight is deceiving, Aífe. By nightfall, it will be cold out here in the wind. Let's erect our shelter and prepare our camp."

They pushed the poles into the sand, leaning them against the cliff face, and then they draped an oiled tarp over the poles with a few stones to weight the leather against the wind. A second tarp made a floor to keep out the sand. Finally, they gathered stones to make a round cooking hearth. Bébinn would spend her days collecting driftwood and dried seaweeds for the fire while Aífe accomplished her tasks.

"Are you growing tired of all this instruction yet?" Bébinn asked as they put the finishing touches to their camp.

"No, I am actually glad I came to this place," Aífe replied truthfully, humming softly to herself as she unpacked the last of her things.

Bébinn had no doubt that the presence of the handsome young arrival had something to do with Aífe's pleasant mood.

"It is very nice to hear you singing a little tune to express yourself. The task you have come here for today is to learn to use your voice to accomplish much more. There are many aspects to the sounds that come from your throat. The human voice can chant, sing, and magnify self-expression and creativity. The throat can also be used to achieve power in diplomacy, ambassadorship, and political persuasion. A voice can communicate truth and promote justice, loyalty, and kindness, or it can foster ignorance by misleading and manipulating. It is a powerful tool. There is a deeper mystery involving speech, which is that the spoken word actually shapes reality."

"What do you mean, it 'shapes reality'?" Aífe asked.

"Each time you take in a new awareness or a new bit of knowledge, it influences your thinking. To utter your new knowledge as words, you first have to pattern that knowledge into your thinking. When you express the new idea or awareness out loud, it influences the shape of the world and becomes a self-fulfilling prophecy. In other words, thought and language create reality, and the reality we experience is actually a mirror of the thoughts, language, and speech we have put into play.

"This means that we must pay careful attention to the way we and others use language. Words that remove guilt, shame, and remorse show pure intent. A kind voice that rises and falls like a melody will draw others like a flower draws bees and indicates heartfelt concern in the speaker. A true voice speaks words that nourish our connection to the whole, the entire tribe, to all life. It reminds us of the numinous spirit within all things. Such a voice shows us how to best serve all creation. A voice like that, properly used, can even destroy illness and disease."

"Ethne once sang a dying person to the Otherworld," Aífe observed. "It was as if her song removed pain and brought peace at a terrifying time."

"Exactly. A voice can be used to release tension, to foster love and forgiveness, and bring relaxation and nourishment to the soul. It can be used to communicate these things to others. But the opposite is also true. A voice raised in anger can wound like a sword, and such wounds are often permanent. Harsh words can cause a cut that is carried for a lifetime.

"There is yet another use of the voice that involves power and persuasion. To develop that voice, you must learn to speak with authority, to large as well as small crowds, which is why I brought you to this place. Do you see that cliff over there, opposite to the one where we made our shelter?"

"Yes, I see it," Aífe answered.

"Good. You must stand here by our tent and practice throwing words at that cliff in a normal speaking voice until the sound returns to you as an echo. Then you will know that you have achieved the volume and strength necessary to address a sizeable crowd or to invoke the gods in a large ritual so that everyone can hear you. Use your whole chest to make the words, and send them from the very bottom of your rib cage. And remember to breathe! I will be down on the beach fishing most of the day, in case you wonder where I am."

Aífe practiced all that day and into the next. On the third day, she finally heard the returning echo that told her she had succeeded. Bébinn, who had been sunning herself by the cliff face all morning, heard it too and quickly rose to congratulate her student.

"Excellent work, Aífe, it is much harder for a woman to achieve the voice of authority. Men can often do it in a day because their chests are deeper and larger. I am so very proud of you!"

"Thank you," Aífe said, feeling a little hoarse.

Bébinn reached into her pocket and ceremoniously took out yet another stone.

"This is a stone known as *turcait*, which comes from the east. The sky blue color corresponds to the pool of energy in the throat. You can lay the stone over your throat to soothe and heal it. You can also keep it in your crane bag and simply visualize its color on any red, sore, or inflamed body part, because the color blue helps to release tension and inflammation in the body.

"Visualizing the color blue also allows a person to relax his or her mind and take in feelings of love and forgiveness. You will know it is working when tears flow in a release of pain. You can imagine yourself or another person enveloped in a cloud of blue, and use the color to send healing and love to yourself or to any creature. Can you do that?"

Aífe answered, "I will place the stone on my throat and see myself bathed in a sky blue mist. It will help me to relax my throat muscles after all the yelling I have been doing!"

"Perfect. I'll roast the fish I caught this morning, and then we can break down our camp and go home." And Bébinn neatly draped the filleted fish over a green stick suspended between two Y-shaped branches on either side of the embers.

35

Lucius and Aífe had begun a hidden, silent courtship in the very midst of their training. They stole glances in the evenings around the central hearth, and on the rare occasions when they passed each other on a forest trail, their eyes kindled a fire that neither dared give voice to. It was a secret pleasure shared only by smiles and wondering looks as slowly and inexorably the spark of their first meeting grew into a steady flame.

Both were thoroughly dedicated to their studies, but, despite the warnings of their teachers, each carried the image of the other in a hidden recess of their mind. It was as if a sweet melody played in the background of their awareness, never quite forgotten. Because they had both arrived on the island under strange circumstances, each felt that their meeting was a minor miracle, a part of the gods' plan, and every night as they lay on their separate beds they wished the other well and wondered how the other was progressing in his or her tasks.

One afternoon, Aífe stared into the middle distance as she crouched on the ground, abstractedly grinding wheat berries in a quern that sat on the grass before the women's house. She was remembering the lesson of *cride* and imagining a private afternoon with Lucius in the flower-scented forest clearing when she was brought back to reality by a very businesslike voice.

"Aífe," said Bébinn crisply. "Pack your things for another stay out-of-doors."

They rolled up their extra clothing and tarps, but this time also hung sharp hatchets from their belts. They would need these to cut saplings to fashion a small round hut twined with leaves and bark against the rain. Bébinn also brought a shovel. They walked through the woods to a huge slab of bare rock just north of the Druid settlement. The rock lay at a steep angle and was perched high enough so that by sitting on top one could see above the tree line.

They spent the first day gathering saplings, placing the butt end of each one into a hole and bending it towards the ground to fix the opposite end into a hole about eight feet away. The eventual result was a beehive structure into which they wove more saplings and leafy branches in and around the sides, to make it waterproof. Then they built a shallow, wide cooking pit outside of the shelter by lining a square of clay soil with flat stones and building up a wall of flat stones around the edges.

Bébinn planned to set snares in the forest to collect small game while Aífe practiced her assignment. The game would be cleaned and gutted, wrapped in grasses, and set to boil in the pit, which would be filled with water. She would bring the water to boil by dropping in rocks heated to a red glow in the fire.

The fire pit was added last, constructed under a slight overhang of rock to protect it from the rain. When everything was ready for a long stay, the instructions began.

"Today's lesson is called *súil inmedónach*. It is the test of inner vision and inner sight. We have already talked about serpent wisdom. This lesson is another aspect of that way of knowing," Bébinn said.

They clambered to the top of the projecting rock and settled themselves into the ancient cross-legged seated posture, with each foot resting on the opposite thigh.

"Start by putting your hands in the usual gesture of concentration; curl your forefinger into the tip or first joint of your thumb and extend the other three fingers, and let your hands rest open upon your thighs."

Aífe had a lifetime of meditation practice and settled herself easily.

"Now close your eyes and open them again, just slightly. Bring your awareness to the middle of your forehead, between your eyes, just above the root of your nose. Can you find the spot?"

"Yes, I feel as if my body has made a triangle with the point between my eyes as the top and my crossed legs as the base," Aífe replied.

"Exactly right. Your body should be as relaxed and centered as if you were a sack of grain. When you pick up a grain sack from the top, all the weight falls to the base. That relaxed stability gives your mind the freedom to center and focus.

"When you concentrate on your third eye, the point between your eyebrows, you automatically bring energy there. Do this whenever emotions threaten to overwhelm you or when you need to gain the altitude to contemplate a problem dispassionately. The third eye is the witness, the part of you that watches your thoughts, hears your words, and notices what you are choosing to see or focus on at any given moment.

"I know that you have experienced the *imbas*, the sudden flash of poetic insight. *Imbas* can happen at random—for example, during meditation or when we are just falling asleep or upon waking. But if you learn to focus on your third eye, you can consciously work with *imbas*, see the Otherworld, and receive its messages at will. An opened third eye will also allow you to better sense the gods, the *Sidhe*, and the land spirits and see their pathways in the landscape.

"You must develop this skill in order to function effectively as a Ban-Drui; otherwise, emotion might cloud your judgment. As Druid, we must be deeply grounded and keep a strong connection to everyday reality, even as our heads are in the sky world. Do you understand?" Bébinn asked.

"Oh, yes, I do. Ethne calls that oak wisdom—having your roots deeply in the ground while your branches are in the sky, attracting the lightning and attention of the gods. All the while you must be strong enough to feed the people, as the oak does with its nuts; warm the people, as the oak does with its firewood; and provide the people medicine, just as the oak does with the gift of its leaves and bark." Aífe remembered the lectures she had heard on this subject at the Forest School while sitting under the large oak tree.

"Ethne often told us that unless we could find something reflected in nature, it simply was not true. 'Three candles illumine every darkness: truth, nature, knowledge,' she liked to say."

"She is a wise one, your Ethne," Bébinn observed. "On a spiritual level, an open third eye will aid you in finding forgiveness and in letting go of anger and resentment, because it gives you altitude and perspective on life's trials that fosters nobility and generosity of spirit. An open third eye also dissolves false conditioning and ingrained habits of thinking.

"Bringing your awareness to your third eye also helps in problem solving. Seeing the world through the lens of the third eye shows you a third way when you are debating two opposite ideas. It will help you find an answer that you had not thought of when you are caught between two opposite choices.

"Use your third eye to practice transcendence, to control your ego and mind. And as you watch your thoughts, notice what your focus is on. Are you focusing too much on your self, your own welfare? Are you forgetting the needs of the tribe, of the whole of life?

"As a woman, you are well aware of the monthly cycle of the moon and the cleansing that happens through the shedding of blood. Use this practice to purify and renew your mind and your spirit, just as your shed blood purifies your body. If you do this practice diligently, it will also give you the psychic ability to see auras and foresee the future."

Bébinn left her then on the perch of rock poised between land and sky.

Aífe practiced for many hours until she achieved a deep trance state. Hunger and thirst no longer mattered. Each time she felt a pang, she returned her awareness to that central point between her eyebrows. The smell of Bébinn's cooking did not move her, so strong was her focus. A full moon rose in the east, casting deep shadows from the treetops onto the surface of the stone upon which she was seated, but Aífe did not see it, so deep was her inner gaze.

At one point she had a vision of seeing Lucius, but it wasn't quite him. At first the figure she saw was dressed in princely garb. Then she saw him again, dressed in a coarse brown robe and singing or chanting with a large group of men, also dressed in brown. The image was so vivid it was a lucid dream, brighter and stronger than waking reality. She jolted back to awareness of the hard stone beneath her, still radiating faint warmth from the afternoon sun.

"Aífe, it is time to come down now!" Bébinn was calling from below.

As they sat by the fire, Aífe told Bébinn what she had seen. Bébinn took in her words but did not comment and handed Aífe a wooden bowl of rabbit stew.

"Try not to dwell on your vision. It will make sense over time," was all Bébinn said.

At dawn, after they had woken and washed their faces in a nearby brook, Bébinn took yet another stone from her pocket. It was dark blue, with tiny flecks of silver and white shot through it.

"This is yet another gift for your crane bag. It is lapis, the indigo stone that opens the light of the inner eye and protects inner wisdom and judgment."

"It is like the night sky filled with stars!" said Aífe, delighted.

She spent three more days and nights practicing bringing her awareness to her third eye while holding on to the indigo stone.

36

Lucius had flawlessly passed the test of power. That evening, after Amalgáid and Lucius returned to the Druid settlement from the Eagle's Beak, Lucius lay on his bed in the men's house.

How strange it would be if Teilo and Justan could see me now, he thought. *How little they know of the world! Their thoughts are shaped entirely by the teachings of the schola at Inissi Leuca. They have no idea that other gods and goddesses, other paths to the divine, even exist. For them, the ancient teachings are blasphemy, ugly, something to be avoided at any cost.*

He felt suddenly sad for the brothers and monks who were missing out on so much beauty, and he felt especially bad for Martinus and his misguided minions who chopped down trees and destroyed sacred wells and sanctuaries. He felt sorry for those whose religion was circumscribed by a written book.

Why can't they lift their noses out of that book and see the sacred creation all around them? The divine is so much larger than books. No one book could possibly describe or contain the miracles that happen every day, like the fact that the sun rises each morning and the flowers know when to close at night... Then the exertions of the day finally overtook him, and he drifted off into a peaceful sleep.

Amalgáid was at the Main House seeking a sounding board, someone with whom to discuss his appraisal of Lucius. He thoroughly approved of the sober charge who weighed his actions so carefully before speaking or acting, a trait Amalgáid respected. The young man was profoundly inner-directed and not easily moved by the agendas of others.

Báetán bustled about the Main House like a bee, energetically pursuing his labor of bringing in armloads of firewood and stacking them neatly against a wall.

"Báetán, stand still for a moment so I can share something with you," Amalgáid said.

Báetán placed the last stick on the pile that now reached nearly to the thatched roof and turned to give Amalgáid his full attention.

"Our student is precocious, a deep soul with great potential. Today I read his aura and his spirit, and I saw something rather surprising. I need your opinion."

"Certainly. What did you see?"

"I saw into his past, or maybe it is his future—it's hard to be sure. He comes from a noble line; there was a golden torc about his neck. Very odd for one who came to us looking like a half-drowned wharf rat, don't you think?"

Báetán replied, "If you saw it, dear Amalgáid, it is a true vision. Your Sight rarely deceives you. These are strange times, and many changes are afoot on the mainland. It would not surprise me if the gods had sent us a future leader of the tribes. So many things now hang in the balance."

"I suppose you are right. The fact that there are two of them is fascinating, is it not?" Amalgáid asked.

"We will have to be patient and see what the future brings. From what Bébinn says, the young woman is equally talented," Báetán responded.

"Perhaps it is a special grace from the High Ones. Maybe they have sent us two especially strong souls to carry on the old ways in the midst of the destruction all around us," Amalgáid mused.

He reached for a silver jug of the Waters of Life, kept high on a shelf for ceremonial and medicinal use, and poured a thin stream into the fire as a thanks offering to the unseen ones who had sent such promising charges, and watched as blue tongues of flame licked towards the smoke-blackened opening by the roof-tree, bearing his offering up to the sky.

"*Is buide lemm frit,*" he murmured reverently. "Thank you for your gifts to us."

37

We will not be returning to the Druid settlement again until you have finished all your lessons," Bébinn announced over a breakfast of fried mushrooms and pan bread one morning. "We will be out here for some time."

Aífe pensively swallowed the last of a cup of wild peppermint tea and mentally prepared herself for still-harder tests to come.

"That tea is the last food or drink you will take for the next four days—if you choose to go on with your lessons, that is," said Bébinn.

"Four days?" Aífe asked with a small shiver of fear.

Aífe was genuinely scared. It was a long time to go without food or water; maybe she would die this time. But she knew that she was free to decide whether to go on or not.

"It is your decision. You can stop your training now and you will be considered an advanced *ban-fili*," Bébinn said.

Aífe swallowed hard, staring into her empty cup, thinking and hoping that the swirl of peppermint leaves lying at the bottom might provide some mystical guidance.

Bébinn was unsure whether the young woman had the courage to go on and held her breath, silently awaiting her decision.

Finally Aífe spoke. "I choose to continue. I don't want to quit before I have finished all my tests."

Bébinn exhaled in relief.

"That's exactly what I hoped you would say. Good; let's climb up to the rock again and resume your lessons."

Bébinn was proud of the girl; not everyone continued the rigors of training to the very end. "We will start by casting a ring of protection around you and this rock," she said, producing a bag of vervain and a packet of salt from a leather purse that hung from her belt. "Take the vervain and make a circle of purification with it. You will live within the circle you define for the next four days. Be sure it reaches to the very edge of the rock so you can release your bodily fluids when you have the need."

Aífe made a thin circle of vervain that reached to the very edge of the precipice.

"Now take this bag of salt and make a second circle within the circle of vervain. The salt will help you to concentrate and will keep away any baneful spirits."

Aífe made the second circle just inside of the green circle of dried herbs.

"Now call in the spirits of the directions to sanctify the space in which you will dwell for the next four days."

Aífe called in the battle-eagle of the north, the wise salmon of the east, the deep-rooting boar of the south, and the noble stag of the west. Lastly, she called the mare of sovereignty, the spirit of rulership and self-mastery, into the sacred center.

Bébinn continued. "Just as when the gods brought you near this island and none of us could tell if you would be accepted by coming around the rock *dessel*, so this vigil will establish your firm relationship with your guardian spirits. No one can say if the spirits will make themselves known to you or if you will be given a message to guide you on your path. But it is very important that you try."

Aífe sat down in the center of the magical ring, and Bébinn handed her the woolen blanket that would be her only protection from the elements.

"Do you remember how you heard a voice soon after you arrived in the women's house and you had the vision of three balls of flame?

Hopefully your guardian spirit will be with you here. He or she will tell you your true name and reveal many other secrets. This is the lesson of *saidecht*, and if you succeed, it will give you perfect self-mastery. I will never be far from here. I will stay in the hut at the base of this rock to guard and protect you. But you must remain within the circle of salt and vervain until four days and nights have passed."

"What about the cold?" Aífe asked.

"Use your third eye. You have the skill to transcend the cold," Bébinn responded firmly, disappearing over the lip of the rock even as she uttered the words.

Now Aífe was alone; the stone on which she sat and the vast sky were her only company.

Mantra is the way. The words of her teacher Ethne drifted suddenly into her awareness.

She sat with crossed legs in the pose of balance and intoned the sacred syllable *Om* handed down from when the ancestors came from the East into the forested wilderness of the island. She pronounced it "Ah-OO-MM," in the way she had been taught.

She moved her awareness to her third eye and immediately shifted into trance. At once a vision arose. Five symbols or objects moved quickly in a sunwise spiral as a voice said:

"Behold earth, air, fire, water, and ether.
Always in motion,
Destroying and re-creating each other
In an endless dance."

The circle moved faster and faster until it made her dizzy. It looked as if earth were attempting to smother water, water was trying to drown fire, fire was heating air and burning it up, air was trying to blow away everything before it, ether was pushing, pushing to keep the circle in motion … the chase grew even faster and more violent, like a rabid dog madly chasing its own tail.

She stepped mentally into the exact center of the melee.

All motion stopped.

"There is nothing going on," said the voice. "It is all illusion. The elements are the same as your five senses. You can choose to step away from those at any time; cold, heat, happiness, sorrow, desire—they are all the same. You can choose to feel them, to focus on them, or not. You are a spirit inhabiting a place of endless conflict. But you don't have to identify with it, unless you choose to. This is the gift of self-mastery. Once you know this, you can overcome any disease or the effects of any poison. Step away from the endless battle within the world, within your own body and mind."

After, it took no effort to sit hour after hour. She had entered a peaceful, timeless void. When the cold night came, she endured it and found it was no worse than the heat of the *tech ind allais*, the sweat house where she had often withstood the baking temperature of the stones. She had entered the opposite, a house of cold. She found that by shifting her awareness to her extremities—fingers, feet, and toes— she could warm them at will.

She emerged from her trance at times, sometimes in the full sun of daylight or under the lush light of the summer moon. As the days wore on, she became aware of a sweet chorus of song that permeated the air, a song in an ancient tongue, beautiful to the ears but impossible to decipher. The singers, whoever they were, sang in perfect three-part harmony, never faltering or missing a note.

"You are hearing the song of the earth, the song of creation," the spirit voice breathed into her inner ear. "This is the ancient song that the fairies sing to bring plants, animals, and minerals into form, the song through which they sing the world into being. Only those who have stilled their mind and body can hear the song, yet it is eternal and ever-present.

"Would you like to know your true name?" the voice asked, in a tone as deep and melodious as lake water.

"Yes," she replied.

She saw a flower with a blazing light in its center. All around the flower were dark skies, thunder, and lightning.

"The light within the rose, the light within the windstorm," said the voice. And Aífe knew it was her true, eternal name.

Then she heard a voice calling, a fully human voice from far away. It was Bébinn, calling her back to the material world.

"Here, drink this," Bébinn said, suddenly beside her, handing her a cup of mashed berries and pure spring water. Aífe had never tasted anything so delicious. She slowly and carefully savored the liquid, sip by sip.

"There is more of this drink waiting for you below, and there are hazelnuts and apples to break your fast."

At length Aífe found her legs and slowly crawled down from the rock to find that Bébinn had laid out a feast of fruits and nuts before a blazing fire. Aífe could still hear the song of the earth as she told Bébinn everything she had seen and heard. Gradually, as food, warmth, and sleep overtook her, the song faded into memory, never to be forgotten.

When Aífe was rested and fully awake, Bébinn handed her a cut sea-green *beirel* for her crane bag. "This is the stone that neutralizes all poisons," Bébinn said, and Aífe understood, nodding her head in silent thanks.

38

The next day, Bébinn said it was time to once again take up Aífe's instruction. "For this lesson, we must walk to a very special hill at the north end of the island."

Aífe no longer felt fear or reservation. She had mastered the elements and knew she could transcend the needs of her body. "Is this fearlessness a permanent state of mind?" she asked Bébinn. "Or will I forget when I am back on Ériu and dealing with life's challenges once again?"

"You will always have these experiences as strength to draw upon if you but choose to remember them. They are a storehouse for the rest of your life. They will even stay in your memory when you are reborn in future lives. Your mind may not consciously remember, but your spirit will always know these things."

Aífe was content, saying nothing more as they trekked their way through the woods to the hill in the north. When they reached it, Aífe saw that it was not really a hill but rather a large knob of stone that towered over the trees. They climbed its gentle slope easily and stood together at the summit, peering out in all directions. The view was magnificent.

"I can see the ocean on every side and the whole island spread around me like a carpet!" said Aífe, marveling. She saw the south beach where she had first landed, the Druid settlement with its earthen ramparts, and all the way up to the shore beyond the hill on which they stood, to the northern tip of the island. She had never had such a vantage point before—it was like standing over a three-dimensional map.

"This must be the way the gods see all of creation. They look at us creatures and hold us all in their sights. The vast sea and the waves around this island are like the great Ocean of Being—raw energy and power not yet manifested as form. The waves come into shore inexorably to create life and change," said Aífe.

"How do you feel as you take in the entire island at once?" Bébinn asked.

"I feel great love and affection, not only for the people below but for every inch of the island: its plants, its trees, its animals, the invisible nature spirits, even the wind and the stones. It's all equally sacred to me and equally beloved. I can feel the divine essence within everything I see."

"Very good. You have reached the spiritual plane of divine love for all beings. This experience is called *corann*, because divine love rises from the crown of your head like an umbilicus to your higher self, which is actually connected to the higher self of all creatures, like the petals of a great flower."

"Yes, it's as if there is only one great Being with no separation. Now I understand that the divine exists like a seed within every speck of creation. I feel a divine union with all forms of life and existence: mineral, plant, animal, human, spirits, and gods. It is all One," Aífe said, with wonder in her eyes.

Bébinn reached into her pocket and produced a beautiful piece of *ametis* for Aífe's crane bag. It was filled with color and fire.

"You have no need of these baubles any more, but perhaps one day, when you are sorely tested, they will help to re-anchor these experiences in your mind."

"Oh, Bébinn, these gifts from your hand are precious to me. I will never forget the lessons you have given me!" Her eyes filled with tears as she looked at Bébinn, who now appeared as a goddess, ineffably beautiful, with eyes that blazed love and a divine fire that illuminated her face.

"There is one more secret I must share with you on this sacred island that mimics all of creation."

"There's more?" Aífe was thunderstruck. How could there be more magic than the god-consciousness she had just experienced?

"Focus on your heart as I speak," Bébinn said. "What do you see with your inner eye?"

Aífe turned her vision inward to her beating heart. "I see a white flower."

"Tell me what it is doing."

"It is slowly unfolding, one petal at a time, filling my body with light."

"How do you feel as it does this?"

"Like a still pool under a cloudless sky on a high mountaintop, with no up or down, nothing to strive for, and nothing to do or say. I am at one with everything."

"Excellent. This is the station called *solus*, where your physical form diffuses like a cloud. There is nothing beyond this. Once you are in this state, being is enough. It is a place of bliss, the abode of the Goddess Mother within all creation. There is no physical part of your body connected to this awareness, but there is a pool of energy called the Soul Star that rises above your head. Once your Soul Star is awakened, the world becomes endlessly beautiful and every second of life, no matter where you are, appears as a precious miracle, a gift. The world is your food, the ambrosia of the gods, and you are drunk with it.

"Within this feeling of bliss there is a great mystery. In the center of the great ocean of being is an island of nine gems. This island is your body and also all creation, where life rises and falls in and out of existence like the waves at your feet. You see the divine in everything and know all things are possible because you are supported by the divine within and without. You will never again push the waves because no matter what happens, you will know that the universe is unfolding as it should and that all things will come to you in their time.

"Never again will you accept spiritual intimidation from anyone. You know that you and they are equally divine, and if you but remember this, you will never again have need of fear or guilt. Your life will be devoted to cultivating joy and serenity in yourself and on behalf of others.

"As a symbol of this state of awareness and peace, I have one last gift for your crane bag." Bébinn pulled out a spear of *cristall glain*, flawless, without blemish, and shot through with rainbows of refracted light.

"Use this stone to focus your will, as a tool of manifestation. Now that your Sight is pure, you will act on behalf of the highest good of all creation. I know this to be so."

"What if I get off-track? It is so easy to be blissful here, where everything and everyone conspires to aid me. But I know that it won't be easy to keep this inner peace when I leave the shores of this place." Aífe was already thinking of the world beyond Innis nan Druidneach and of the potential challenges and distractions she would inevitably face there.

"You will know you have gone astray if you experience sadness, sickness, anger, fear, or grief, or if there is a breakdown of any of your bodily organs. When that happens, you must return to the state of innocence and see the world again through each of the states of awareness you felt here on the island, until you re-experience joyful union with all existence."

"That is a lot to ask. I know that at some point I will become angry or sad," Aífe said.

Bébinn smiled. "You are allowed to be angry for as long as a line can be drawn upon water. Then you must bless the divinity within whatever or whomever has pushed your patience."

Aífe looked far below at the surface of the sea. She imagined a staff in her hand, etching a line through the silver blue, and saw how quickly the shifting water swallowed the mark. She smiled, looked at Bébinn, and said simply, "I understand."

They came down from the hill to dismantle their little camp, looking forward to a hot bath and all of the comforts of the women's house.

39

When Lucius had at last finished his tasks, both he and Aífe were declared full initiates of Innis nan Druidneach, and everyone was called to the Main House for a celebratory feast.

Dáiríne had outdone even herself, baking enormous deer-meat pies flavored with mushrooms, wild carrots, sea salt, and garlic. Beside the pies was a huge wooden salad bowl filled with watercress, dandelion leaves, and other edible shoots and flowers.

Báetán brought out his very best batch of *mid*, a frothy and not-too-sweet barrelful flavored with rowan berries.

Amalgáid settled himself on a stool before the blazing hearth with a harp in his lap and sang an ancient lay that summarized everything Aífe and Lucius had recently experienced:

> *I am a wave on the windy sea*
> *Over land and sea I am the wind*
> *I am the eagle on the cliff*
> *I am the stone within the mountain*
> *I am the salmon in the forest pool*
> *I am the strength of the boar in rut*
> *I am the tines of the mountain stag*
> *I am the bravery of the wild bull*
> *I am the flower in bloom*

I am the seed within the flower
I am the grain that feeds the people.

I am a word of magic
I am the strength within the strong
I am the silence within the secret
I am the knowledge within the knower
I am the enchanted point of a battle spear
I am the radiant sun of light
I am the stars in the cauldron of sky
I am the ages of the moon.

My word brings the world into being
I grow the shady wood
I release the cleansing waterfall
I hold the pool of the lake
I raise the lofty green meadow
I am the well in the hill
That nourishes the people.
I am the people
I am the past
I am the future
I am the sacred land
I am the sea and the sky … [3]

Aífe had heard the song at Druid gatherings in the past, but never had the words meant so much. Though she and Lucius were at last free to speak to one another, they found it hard to find words in such a public place. With a silent, beckoning glance, Aífe asked Lucius if he would like to go outside to the privacy of the night. They exited the roundhouse together, relieved to be away from the others. But when they were finally alone and far enough from the door that no one would hear their words, they suddenly had none.

Lucius paced a few steps away, turned, and opened his mouth to speak, but when he saw Aífe in the moonlight, his thoughts bunched in his throat. Aífe tried to use the calming technique of *súil inmedónach* but could gain no altitude of mind; nothing inside of her was still. Finally, Lucius motioned her to a stone wall, where they sat and pretended to listen to the crickets and the night animals rustling in the leaves.

"Are you happy here?" Lucius burst out in desperation.

"Oh, yes." Aífe opened her hands for emphasis. "This place holds more than happiness for me."

Lucius nodded agreement but said no more.

"And you?" Aífe blushed at her clumsiness.

Lucius searched for words so long, Aífe thought he would not answer. Just as the silence was impossible to bear, he said, "I have never been home before."

Aífe turned fully toward him, her face turned up and questioning. It was not what she had expected him to say. Before she could ask or give answer, Lucius hurried on.

"I don't know who I am, you see. I'm no one's, and I belong nowhere. The odd thing is, I didn't really know that until I came here and found that I belong to myself."

It all came out in a tumble, and his breath came as if he had been running.

Aífe reached for his hand and took it in both of her own. "Now you belong everywhere," she said.

He looked up and found her eyes waiting for him. "What did you find here in this place?"

Aífe's smile came readily. "I found everything—everything I will ever need."

"Yes, I feel that way too," he said.

They sat in quiet now, a softly rocking balance moving between them. Slowly, Aífe moved one hand away and curled it through Lucius's arm. She felt his warmth and his strength. "I have a family," said Aífe. Her words came slowly. "But they are not the mother and father that bore me. The family I have is loving, kind, and open. They have made me forget that I was not originally from them. A child should know that they are wanted, that they bring a gift that no other can bring. I am sorry that you have been so alone."

Lucius's heart thudded in his chest and a single warm tear escaped his eye. He pulled his arm tight to his side to hold Aífe there more firmly. He knew she needed no answer. Instead, he stood, she beside him as they walked the pine-covered path under the trees. The movement brought him ease, and she too needed the steps beside him to express her feelings. She let her arm drop and found his hand. He brought hers up to his mouth and kissed it. She stopped and let him feel the tug on his arm. She was a step away from him. He turned, not knowing why she had stopped, saw her face framed in the night. Before he could form a thought, he scooped her to him and caught her mouth in a small, surprised "Oh!" And then they were together, he bending slightly over her, capturing her to his chest, his heart hammering full of unbelieving joy. Aífe reached to him, tangled her hands in his hair, and held to his love.

When they finally parted, they stood staring at each other as if this were the moment they had always expected and as if nothing could have stunned them more. Lucius hesitated, bent, and placed a warm, firm kiss on her lips, pulled back a fraction, and whispered, "I am home."

In silence, they sank to the forest floor and explored every known and unknown hollow and ridge of their excitement, their wonder, their bodies, their love. An urgent need drove them. Without thinking, Lucius lifted up Aífe's robe, and she returned the gesture, tearing his clothes off in a moment. He held the softness of her breasts and found the heat of her sex, bringing himself to her. She met him in his passion, caressing the muscles of his back, holding the excitement of his loins until they shuddered, cried out, and moaned together into the deep night. When Lucius raised himself to look at Aífe, she laughed.

"What's so funny?"

"Nothing. Everything! I didn't know I could hold so much happiness!" She half rose, kissed his neck, rose more, and bit him slightly on the lip. He could not resist and let himself be drowned again.

They lay flat on their backs and stared up at the stars. Neither spoke. Then Lucius said, "The moon has traveled far on our little walk."

Aífe giggled. "Is that your way of telling me we have gone too far?"

Lucius laughed. "No, but I suppose it is my way of saying maybe we should go back. The others may be worried."

When they re-entered the Main House with rumpled tunics, hand in hand, it was perfectly clear to the Druid why the gods had led them there together. Bébinn brought them *mid* and a loaf of honey bread to share, saying with a smile, "The night air makes one hungry." Talk and song swirled around them, and Aífe and Lucius were allowed their privacy.

The next day, Aífe woke early. As she sat up, she hugged her happiness to herself, and a shiver ran through her body. She thought of Lucius, how he belonged in her heart, how he was like the elemental land, sea, and sky that kept her alive. And then she thought of Ethne and Ruadh. They believed in her and needed her. She was not alone on this quest.

She walked to the Main House and found Lucius in conversation with the others.

"Amalgáid, when and how does one leave this place?" Lucius asked. "The season of winter is approaching, and we must make the crossing before the storms set in."

"You are free to leave whenever you like. We will arrange a passage for you when the next boat arrives, bringing our winter supplies. The winds have already shifted, and the balmy southern breezes no longer caress the shore. Often now the winds are bitter cold, more and more frequently blowing in from the snow-lands in the north. If you are to go, it must be soon."

Lucius gave Aífe a questioning glance and beckoned her to follow him outdoors. They retraced their steps down the forest path where their love had been sealed and discussed the future, two heads bent together as one under the arching pines. They had many options before them: to stay on the island and join the community separately or together, or to return to Gallia or to Ériu, each alone or as a pair.

The packet ship arrived the very next day from the mainland, bringing mail, skeins of wool, and a few sacks of wheat. The community offered *mid* and honey in exchange for these necessities, and the captain of the boat was invited to stay the night.

That evening at supper, Amalgáid proposed a toast: "To our most unusual students—in this tumultuous time, it has been our distinct honor to serve you both."

Everyone raised their cups, and Aífe spoke. "Ethne, Ruadh, and Gaine sent me here not for myself but for all the Forest Druid. This is not my quest alone; it belongs to them too. They have risked everything over and over to keep the old ways safe. Now it is my turn to take up the task. Lucius and I have been through all the tests and initiations. We may yet grow to be great *fili* like you, Bébinn, Amalgáid, Dáiríne, and Báetán. But we are meant to do it in the world together, as a pair, Lucius and I."

Lucius added, "I was raised to be a *Cristaide* priest, and most of them are celibate. But I have learned that the single life is not for me; I want a woman in my life. We have the right, the free will to make our own decisions—the lessons of this island have taught us that much, and we have decided to go out into the world hand in hand."

Aífe thought of her days on the rock and of the new strength inside her, the freedom and power to make her own way. She gripped Lucius's hand tightly. "I have never been in love before."

Lucius pulled her to him. "We are for each other, Aífe, the gods have willed it so. Why else would they have sent us here together?" he kissed her lightly on the cheek.

"We welcome your decision; it comes as no surprise," said Bébinn, laughing.

Lucius and Aífe looked around the room at the smiling, loving faces.

"You knew?" Aífe asked.

"We did!" Amalgáid exclaimed. "We have simply been waiting for you to make your choice."

"Let's pour out some more of this excellent *mid*, shall we?" said Báe-tán, dancing around the pair, waving cups in one hand and offering a brimming pitcher full from the other. And they sang and danced into the night, as at a marriage feast.

40

Where do we go now? Neither of us has blood kin," Aífe asked Lucius as the embers from the hearth of the Main House were being banked and smoored for the night. "Where do we go to be handfasted?"

"The monks of Inissi Leuca told me that I came from a fishing family on the coast, but I don't know if I believe it. The families there are all dark, and I look nothing like them. I have searched for my clan for years but have had no luck finding them."

Aífe took his hands in hers to comfort him; it seemed they were more alike than either had realized. "I also lost my parents when I was a baby. They were Druid; they died in a fire after a raid by the men of the north. I was raised by Ethne and Ruadh in the Forest School, and the Ard-Ban-Drui, Gaine, has been like a grandmother to me. We could go to them."

And so it was decided. They hired the little packet boat to take them the short distance to the northern kingdom of the island, and they would make their way south to the *nemed* of the central kingdom and to Gaine.

"Bébinn, I have a question for you before we go," Aífe said as she packed the green woolen robes that would mark her as an initiate of Innis nan Druidneach. "Why is there no fire altar on this island? I have searched everywhere but have found no place of worship, no stone circle, no holy well or sacred tree. How do you do ritual with nowhere set apart as sacred ground?"

"Can't you guess the answer? The whole island is sacred to us. Every pebble, tree, and brook is a place of worship. When we visit the mainland, we feel the same way. There is nothing that exists that is not sacred to us. The whole world is our sacred circle.

"We have no need of formal ritual because every act we do is a form of prayer. We live so that every word and gesture comes from our highest intention for the good of the whole. You might see us drop an offering into fire or water from time to time out of gratitude for the many gifts we have been given, but we don't get any more formal than that. For us our religion is a way of being, not a set of rules or ceremonies.

"Once you are back on Ériu, you will again have need of those things. The main purpose of religion there is to bring the sacred teachings to the people, and they must have the ritual forms. Over time, they too will learn that every season is equally holy, that the earth, fire, and water are holy, that they should behave in a way that shows gratitude for all creation, at all times.

"The people will always need their special holy days and gathering places so they can come together and recognize the sacred in their groups and families. They will need a place to go when they seek reassurance and a place to sanctify their births and deaths. You and Lucius will hold such a place for them where they can come with their problems and be reminded of the divine Source that exists within all."

"Thank you. I understand," Aífe said. Now that they were free to speak about their experiences, Lucius and Aífe were delighted to find that they had undertaken the same tasks at the same power spots on the island. They talked long into the night, further cementing their bond as fellow initiates and lovers.

They left at dawn the next day, bearing greetings for Ethne and Ruadh and a large bag of bee pollen for Gaine, to strengthen her in her illness. They crouched comfortably against the leather side of the small craft and held each other, simply enjoying the sound of each other's breathing, the cries of the gulls overhead, and the sighing wind and lapping waves.

"Aífe, I have very few personal possessions that I can call my own, but I want to give you something, a gift to mark the beginning of our time together." Lucius reached into the leather crane bag that was tied to his belt. From it he took his piece of *cristall grisainech* and pressed it into Aífe's palm.

"I want you to think of my love every time you hold this stone. I often imagined lying with you in the sweet grass of that beautiful little glade in the heart of Innis nan Druidneach. When you hold my stone, think of the flowers and the gentle fawns and my love," he said, planting a soft kiss on her upturned face.

"I had the same vision. When I imagine that little glade, it is the secret sanctuary within my heart, the place where I will go to find inner peace and healing. I will always see you there, waiting for me beside the little stream." Aífe reached into the crane bag that was attached to her belt and took out her own glistening pink stone. Pressing the crystal into his hand, she folded his fingers over it and held his hand until all her love passed through it.

They knew they were in the embrace of something as deep as the surrounding sea.

part three

Keepers of the Sacred Flame

41

By the time Lucius and Aífe reached the court of In Medon, Gaine was already failing. The news had gone out to the kingdoms, and tribesfolk were gathered in dense, sad clusters outside the perimeter of the *nemed*.

Aífe held Gaine's withered hand and stroked her forehead, caressing the aged face as if she were a child.

"Gaine," Aífe said gently, using the words she had been taught by Ethne to ease the passage from this life to the next. "You were sent to this life from the Otherworld, and now it is your time to return from whence you came. Your family and relations are waiting for you in that beautiful land where the apple trees are ever in bloom and where it is always high summer."

But Gaine's gaze was already fixed on something that none could see. "Mother?" she asked in a wondering tone, with an expression of awe on her face, as if she saw a presence at the foot of her bed. And then her head fell suddenly to one side, and all her breath escaped in one long sigh.

A blue spirit light floated out of Gaine's mouth. Everyone saw it. Aífe quickly reached out to capture the globe of light in her hand and carefully held it close to her heart for a moment. Then she released it from her two hands. The globe hovered in midair for a heartbeat, then winked out. Gaine was gone.

Aífe's loss was tempered by Lucius's presence. "At least you got to meet her before she passed over," Aífe said as Lucius reached out his arms to enfold her in a comforting embrace.

A Drui stepped outside and began reciting a long, intricate poem of the transition from this life to the next. The people understood that the end had finally come, and a wail went up from woman to woman—keening that would continue for days.

Máel Ísu was elated at the news of Gaine's death, though he tried not to let his feelings show out of deference to the mourners gathered in the *rath*. Most of them were women.

Typical, he thought. *Only the weak and credulous cling to the blind superstitions taught by the Druid. But I wish they would stop that infernal yowling!* He had not yet spoken with the Ard-Ri, Cadla, about Gaine's death, but he was already issuing orders to the monks.

"Cut down the hedges that separate the *nemed* from the king's enclosure," he said. "Leave that old ash tree because the people are used to gathering under it, and it will attract them to our new chapel. Dismantle the fire altar; it is the center of superstitious nonsense. I don't want people putting offerings into the fire ever again or using it to engender hallucinations."

Gaine's body still lay on her small cot in the hut as Máel Ísu moved to abolish her work. He would not allow the all-night vigil that was customary. He shuddered at the idolatry within the Druid-led burial rites.

"Send her body back to her people," he commanded. "Let them take her to her kin-lands for burial. That will distract the most determined of her followers for a while, and we can begin building in peace."

The elderly women of the *tuath* lovingly washed and dressed Gaine's body, covered it in a shroud, and then placed it on a wooden cart for transport to the kingdom of Torcrad. They twined sprays of flowers and bunches of greenery around the bier and body, and tucked offerings of honey, *mid*, and artemisia brew in and around the blossoms as grave offerings and to help the funeral celebrations of her kin. In a loving touch, her hair was braided with the lavender sprigs she had worn in her younger days.

The protective hedgerow of rowan, hawthorn, and elderberry that had circled the *nemed* for generations was already being hacked to the ground as Cadla emerged from his hall to pay respects to Gaine. A profusion of red berries spilled over the ground, fast being ground to a pulp under the feet of the workers.

Despite the preparations that had gone on for several turnings of the sun, Cadla found it strange to see the destruction of the ancient *nemed*. The kingdom was moving so swiftly into new, uncharted ways. He had anticipated the construction of the new chapel for many sun-cycles but secretly felt there was something dishonorable in the way the old Ard-Ban-Drui had been shunted aside. He still recalled the youthful Gaine of his boyhood, with flowers in her braids and offerings of sweet honey biscuits to go along with her stories and teachings.

"I declare that the Ard-Ban-Drui shall have a full retinue of warriors to escort her to her kinlands, and I myself will ride with them!" he proclaimed loudly from the steps of the Great Hall.

He knew this would please the people and enhance his popularity with the tribes. He had planned the gesture months ago with Máel Ísu. It was a convenient way to distract the people from the construction of the new chapel, and if he was absent when the work started, they could hardly place the blame on him.

A swirl of mourners prepared to follow the cart on foot. Warriors' horses stationed to the sides of the bier shied and sidled impatiently, raising a small cloud of dust. Two carnyx players took their place at the head of the procession, with their curved trumpets gleaming against their saddles.

Cadla was glad that the main roads had been recently refurbished. Now the journey would be unimpeded by ruts and fissures, and the newly cleared roadsides would provide ample space for onlookers. It would be a great display of magnanimity. He had commissioned cooks and provisions to feed the crowds along the way.

All the while, the monks and their hired hands would be busy building the stone chapel in the very heart of the *nemed*.

Lucius and Aífe stayed near the *nemed* to comfort the bereaved, and both planned to follow the funeral procession. Aífe helped the women weave funeral garlands to put around the necks of the horses, and Lucius helped the men fill skins of water for the journey. As Lucius bent down to pour water from a wooden bucket into a large goat-skin, he heard a familiar greeting that came from another place and time:

"*Dominus vobiscum.*"

He spun around. Isidore, Martinus, and Teilo were standing in the harsh sunlight of the courtyard.

"Hah! We knew it was you!" said Teilo, pointing at Lucius's blond curls.

"Thanks be to God, we have him at last," said Martinus, turning his eyes piously towards the heavens before grabbing Lucius by the ear and pulling him to a standing position.

"We have searched high and low for you these many months, from Gallia to Cornubia, and finally here, to the shores of Hibernia! We knew you would turn up sooner or later. You are in terrible trouble with Abbot Mihael. He can't wait to have you back. He told us not to rest until we'd found you."

Martinus was in his glory seeing that the ancient *nemed* was being cleared away. He felt that his proper vocation was destroying the old religion wherever he found it, to purify the land and the people, and make them ready for his god.

"I am a free person," Lucius said. When he straightened, the others stepped back. There was something in his face and the set of his shoulders that told them to be wary. "I will not go back to Inissi Leuca or to the Abbott Mihael. He was kind to me, like a father, but my path now lies elsewhere."

"Do you think you can choose?" Martinus asked. The confidence in Lucius raised a rage in him. "You are nothing. You belong to the monastery and to the brothers who fed you and raised you. Not even the fishermen wanted you. You owe the abbott your life."

Martinus grabbed Lucius's hair and bent his head back as Teilo pinned his arms. "Your place is to serve the monastery, serve us, and do as we charge you. You will instruct these heathens in the true religion. The nobles may have seen the light, but the peasants clearly have not. I recently saw them dancing and drinking at their so-called ritual fires. Look at how they moan over the death of that old witch! And you know better than to talk of free will; such talk is heresy. I think your travels have undone all the good lessons you have been taught. Now you even look like one of these ignorant people! Isidore, call the guards over. I want to make sure that Lucius does not get away again."

They force-marched Lucius into the prisoner's mound, where Cadla's sons, Tanaide and Eógan, took a personal interest in the stranger, installing themselves at the entrance as his guards. Martinus intended to restrain him until the chapel was finished and then escort him personally back to Inissi Leuca. He sent a messenger to Abbott Mihael, informing him that his charge was at last safe.

When the iron gate closed behind him, Lucius felt a surge of rage such as he had never known. He knew that his entrapment would hurt Aífe, and that cut him to the very core. He was livid with Martinus. *He cares nothing for me; he has no respect at all for my person. He has no respect for anyone but himself! Teilo and Isidore are nothing but thugs!* he fumed.

Then Amalgáid's words came into his mind: *You are allowed to be angry for as long as a line can be drawn upon water.*

He used his will to let the rage seep out of him, sending it deep into the earth, to she who can bear and absorb all human troubles. Sitting in the dark, he cocooned within himself, thinking of *súil inmedónach,* the test of inner vision and inner sight. *There's no use wasting energy in useless emotion,* he thought. *I will harbor my strength by going within. I know that there are many kinds of prisons—this mound, an unwanted task, even my own mind and body. None of these can bind me, because my spirit is already free.*

He moved into the ancient cross-legged pose and pushed his awareness to his third eye, transcending his circumstances. He would wait until an opportunity to escape arrived. Then he would act quickly.

42

The procession was well underway before Aífe realized that Lucius was missing. She searched the line of mourners from beginning to end but still could not see him. She was concerned but felt sure she would finally find him when they camped for the night. Someone probably needed his help near the end of the procession, she reasoned. She pushed fear out of her mind by focusing on the needs of those around her.

At dusk, as the travelers stopped to rest and cook lavish meals for the mourners and local villagers, she paced the campfires, seeking Lucius. Surely he would have caught up to her by now. She went from group to group asking, describing him and explaining who he was. No one had seen him. Aífe returned to her own fire and sat poking the embers, trying to answer her questions with logic. Sleep she could not find.

The next day was no different. Lucius did not come, and now Aífe was beside herself. She reached into her crane bag and pulled out the dark blue lapis. "I must remember that the whole universe is around me. There are stars above me and stars below and a great star at the center of the earth. My personal problems are very small ... no more than dust. I must calm my fears and keep my perspective ..."

When the procession reached the border of Torcrad, Rochad, the old Ard-Ri, joined the procession with his formal retinue of twelve mounted warriors and added his own lavish hospitality to the tents, multiplying the wheaten bread, *fion*, and cauldrons of stew and roasted meats that Cadla had already provided. The funeral turned into a spectacle such as had not been seen in a generation or more.

Still Aífe searched.

It took three days to reach the ancient burial grounds of Gaine's kin, a place hallowed by long use, next to the main road where a thick wood of oak surrounded a cleared grassy area, filled with its ancient mounds. In the center was a rectangular tomb of stone that had held the bones of Gaine's ancestors since time began.

The keening grew louder as the tomb came in sight, for the time of final farewells was approaching. Harp players, drummers, singers, and carnyx players gave vent to their grief, sending music soaring to drive out harmful spirits and to honor the deceased. Last offerings were made: sprays of the sacred Golden Bough imported from Letha, haunches of meat, vats of *curmi* and *fion*, and burning braziers of artemisia were placed on the cart that held Gaine's body.

The entire cart was wheeled into the stone enclosure, and, as a final gesture, the horse that had pulled it was sacrificed and laid to rest inside to provide a companion and helper for Gaine in her next life.

When everyone had made their tributes, Cadla strode forward, making sure he was the center of attention by swirling his long purple cape and flashing his silver mail in the sunlight. He wanted to make the most of this very public moment and use his devotion to the old Ard-Ban-Drui to full advantage with the crowd.

He stepped to the entrance of the tomb bearing an expensive length of purple cloth as his personal grave offering. And then he noticed Aífe's blond curls.

He nearly faltered as his attention caught and wandered, his breath stuck in his throat. Aífe, the woman who had scorned him and his offer of queenship, stood there brazenly in the sun. A flame shot up from his thighs to his chest, a fire mixed of rage and lust. His thoughts came fast and tangled. *How dare she stand there in the light of day and show herself before me again, and how much more beautiful than before. I will have her!*

Aífe's attention was distracted. She mourned Gaine's death, and Lucius's disappearance made her turn constantly to scan the crowd. Her back was to the bier.

Cadla reached the funeral cart, hardly knowing what he was about. He dropped the cloth at the foot of the bier, turned, and walked up to Aífe, gripping her arm tightly before she had time to see who had come up beside her.

"You fled once," he hissed into her ear. "You have no protection now." He gritted his teeth and squeezed her arm until she winced, then propelled her towards the bier to bow with him in a final show of respect to Gaine. Aífe did not cry out but composed her face into a mask of calm. Her mind and heart were seething.

Lucius will find me soon, she thought, willing panic away. *This man is a slave to his base emotions. I do not need to play into his drama. All I need to do is keep my dignity and wait. Surely the gods must have a plan.*

She was as good as handfasted to Lucius, and she knew that even a king dare not force her to break such a vow, and she had already faced the test of the terror of the open seas. As long as Lucius was alive, somewhere, she had everything she wanted. She would wait out this unpleasantness. She would endure.

But from then on, Aífe was watched, followed everywhere by guards, and forced to sit at Cadla's feet in the royal tent as he dined with Rochad and members of the *flaith*, all the way back to In Medon.

"What a charming... *consort* you have," said the male *flaith* enviously, not knowing her proper title. The women saw only that she was beautiful and sad.

"She is my concubine," Cadla would answer, loud enough for everyone to hear.

He left bruises on the backs of her arms if she uttered a sound. In former days, she could have sought protection from the Druid, but due to the influence of the *Cristaidi* they had recently been debased to mere magicians in the laws and now had no more status than free farmers. They could no longer exert their influence with the nobles, unless the nobles had a mind to listen.

Aífe's thoughts circled around her situation. *I can't turn to the Cristaidi priests of the new religion since I have no relationship with them, and in any case the Cristaidi do not seem to care much for the dignity of women. They expect a woman to obey a man, no matter the cost, and are even demanding that women be forbidden from carrying weapons, leaving women vulnerable and defenseless.*

I knew that returning to everyday life on the island was going to be a shock and a challenge after my one precious summer on Innis nan Druidneach, but I had not thought it would be this difficult, and so quickly. If I can just stay calm until we get back to In Medon, I will get a message to Ruadh somehow. He will call up the fiana if necessary to save me from this mess.

She was even beginning to wonder if Cadla had deliberately done something to keep Lucius away.

Cadla gathered up costly items of clothing from the noblewomen in the entourage and demanded that Aífe shed her simple green woolen robes and instead wear costly imported silks. The golden jewels he bestowed on her burned her skin like fire. She fought like a *ban-sídaige* at night when he pulled her to him, grinding his pelvis and lips hard against her tender places, pinning down her arms as she lay on the bed.

"Scream this time and you are dead," he said, throwing her to the ground inside their tent, aware that no one could see. But he did not force her, knowing that a rape charge would carry disgrace and loss of face—that much of the old tribal law still dwelled in his conscience.

43

The aged Abbott Germanus hobbled around on his stick, over-seeing with approval the laying of the foundation stones for the new chapel. He could do little more than sit in the sun and murmur his prayers, but he was happy. It was delightful to see his life's work fulfilled and to see the end of the despicable *Pagani* shrine.

Ethne and Ruadh received the official news of Gaine's death by messenger, but Ethne was already aware the moment Gaine passed over. An owl had landed on her open windowsill, hooting and flapping its wings as she was preparing supper.

They left the Forest School in the care of Daire and Clothru and set out for the *rath* of the Ard-Ri. After three days of hard walking, they entered the *rath* easily; most of the available warriors were traveling with the funeral or engaged in building the stone chapel, and there were no guards posted at the gates. They went straight to the *nemed* and gazed in dismay at the shambles.

A few small guesthouses stood at the far reaches of the *nemed*, most of which were now occupied by laborers and monks. One still stood empty because it had a hole in the roof that badly needed thatching. Ruadh collected sally rods to patch the hole while Ethne dug up roots and medicines from the *nemed* garden before they were trampled further under the feet of the workers. She scooped up fallen elder, rowan, and hawthorn berries to dry for later use or to plant at the Forest School.

"Waste nothing" echoed the voice of Gaine in her mind.

She also managed to save the bell branch, still hidden in its rocky recess at the foot of the ruined fire altar. Her hands trembled as she pulled it out, thinking of the proud days when the Druid truths were lived in the open. For a moment, she was overcome with grief at the loss of so much beauty and devotion.

As the former *rígain*, she was allowed to move about as she wished. No one stopped her from gathering simples in the garden. To the warriors and laborers, she was but a sad, middle-aged woman quietly picking at her memories. None suspected the fire that smoldered inside her.

One day, as she walked near the prisoner's mound, she noticed that someone was being kept under guard.

"Who is being held inside?" she inquired of a warrior.

"It's no one important, just a Drui. He is of interest to the *Cristaidi*, so we are ordered to keep him locked up."

Hearing that the prisoner was a Drui, she felt duty bound to visit him and see if he needed anything, perhaps a warm blanket or a hot meal. She was well aware of the conditions within the mound and of the many ways the guards could make a prisoner suffer.

She went back to the guesthouse and prepared a cauldron of soup made with dried deer meat and such herbs as she had from the *nemed* garden. It would serve as dinner for herself and Ruadh that evening, and she would take some to the prisoner.

When the soup was ready, she covered a bowlful of the steaming liquid with a ceramic plate to hold in the warmth, gathered up a coarse linen napkin and a horn spoon, and carefully walked to the mound. As she approached, she saw Cadla's sons sitting at the entrance, playing *fidchell*. They looked up when they finally noticed her.

"What do you have in that bowl?" asked Eógan, wondering if he should be concerned. After all, the woman was a Ban-Drui, and she might be smuggling in a weapon to the hostage.

"It's just a bowl of soup for the prisoner. I know how cold it can get in that cell, especially at night."

"Let me see," said Tanaide, pulling the horn spoon from Ethne's hand and swirling it around in the bowl. When he was satisfied that there was nothing hidden in the soup, he let her pass and fumbled on his belt for the iron key to the gate.

The prisoner sat on a wooden bench in the shadows, so Ethne could not see his face, but his blue robes told her instantly that he was a *fili* from Innis nan Druidneach. The man was of a higher rank than any of the warriors knew. She wondered if Cadla was aware of the true status of the Drui in his custody.

"I salute you in the name of the gods of your people," she said, a formal greeting to let the man know she gave him her respect.

"Thank you for your kind greeting, my lady," he replied politely. "And may your gods be honored always."

Lucius stepped into the light of the opening. The setting sun fell on him, revealing his full face and form.

Ethne dropped the bowl with a cry as soup splattered onto the ground; she stood transfixed. Lucius bent to retrieve the bowl, but she put out her arm to stop him. Without a word, she touched his face, traced the bones of his jaw with her fingers, and looked with wonder into his eyes. Her eyes clouded with tears.

"Crimthann!" Ethne said in a whisper. For before her was Crimthann, her husband, the old Ard-Ri as she had known him in his youth, a reincarnation sent from the Otherworld.

Lucius did not know if she was mad or in some kind of trance. He kept himself very still as he watched the emotions passing rapidly over the woman's face. Ethne stood as if turned to stone, while her tears streamed. She made no move to pick up the forgotten wooden bowl and the little horn spoon.

The princes stared in amazement. "Maybe she is a madwoman?" Eógan asked, suddenly feeling overwhelmed by responsibility. "We had better find her husband!"

They pushed Ethne aside and locked in the prisoner, and then loped off to find Ruadh, who was still perched on top of the guesthouse, tying fat bundles of sally rods onto the wooden frame of the roof.

"Come quickly!" they said. "Your wife has gone mad!"

Ruadh slid to the ground, dropping the thatch from his hands, and followed the princes, who were running back to the mound.

"Oh...my...gods!" he said when he saw the prisoner. He too saw Crimthann brought back to life. "Who are you? And where did you come from?" he asked, still panting.

"I came from Gallia, and then—" Lucius began.

"Who are your people?" Ethne managed to ask.

"I don't know. I was told that I was born to a family of fisher folk on the coast of Armorica, but I have never met them, at least not that I can remember. I was raised by *Cristaidi* monks on the island of Inissi Leuca."

"How old are you?" Ruadh asked

Ethne read the shape of his thoughts and her breathing came hard.

"I am not sure," Lucius answered. "About sixteen turnings of the sun."

Ethne fainted in a crumpled heap at Ruadh's feet.

Lucius bent to help lift Ethne. "Do I frighten her?" he asked.

"It is not fear that freezes her," said Ruadh. "It is recognizing her own blood."

44

ethne and Ruadh ordered the guards to release the prisoner. The former leader of the *fennidi* and the former Ard-Rígain pitched their voices to a tone of absolute authority. Lucius was astounded to observe the effect, even though he had been well schooled at Innis nan Druidneach and remembered vividly the lesson of *fúaimm* and his own voice bouncing back from the cliffs.

They walked to the round house where Ethne and Ruadh were staying and stirred up the banked hearth-fire. Ethne put the cauldron of soup over the fire to reheat, and Ruadh placed three stools in a circle. As Ethne sat down, she took one of Lucius's hands in hers.

"You say you have no kin, but that is not true," she began, with a lump of sadness and joy rising in her throat.

Lucius looked from Ethne to Ruadh and back. He was vibrating with questions, but he knew to wait—knew that he would hear answers that would lead to more questions.

"You have had kin all your life," Ethne continued. "Kin that love you and that have longed for you since the day you were born. You were birthed right here in this *nemed*, to a woman and a man who saw their own deep love in you. Because you were the child of this holy place, you were stolen, and those who loved you thought you were forever lost, drowned at sea."

Lucius took these ideas in, saw the images she painted, and tried to put himself into the story she told.

"Where are my kin now?" he asked.

Ethne let go of his hand and placed her own hands quietly in her lap. "I am your kin," she said. "You are my son."

There was no sound. No one moved.

Without disturbing the silence, Lucius knelt before her and put his hands on either side of Ethne's face. He studied her for a long time, searching her eyes for the childhood that was stolen. He found it in the grieving she had done for her lost child, in the love she had never relinquished for him. He found it in the strength she still had to welcome him home and claim him. He stood, raised her to her feet, and hugged her tightly, then tighter as he swung her off her feet and spun her around and around. "I am your son!" he cried. "I am yours!"

All three were crying, laughing, crying, until the cauldron nearly boiled over and Ruadh had to catch it up quickly off the fire.

"I have never called anyone Mother or Father," said Lucius. "What a strange and wonderful feel they have in my mouth. It is a taste I will never tire of."

Finally they ate, but all the while Ethne did not take her eyes from Lucius.

Ruadh explained to Lucius that his true name was Ruadhán, and that he and Ethne had lost him sixteen turnings of the sun before.

"I thought you were the blood-son of Ruadh when I bore you," Ethne said. "But it is obvious that you are the son of Crimthann, the Ard-Rí." She reached out again, wanting to keep him close. A deep and terrible well in her heart, hidden over with years of scarring, suddenly stirred and overflowed. It was as if the noontime sun shone into every dark recess of her soul.

Lucius took in the story of his birth and slowly absorbed the implications. He was elated, happy to have found his family, and terrified, all at once. "Are you telling me that I am a prince?"

"Yes. You were born to me when I was Ard-Rígain, and the Ard-Ri was your father, though he had crossed to the Otherworld by the time you came into this world. Ruadh has been your foster-father from the first. He was the battle leader of the *fennidi* before he joined me at the Forest School."

"But if you were Ard-Rígain, why did you leave the throne? How did Cadla come to take it?"

"That is a story yet unfolding, my son," Ruadh said. "You were removed from us by the *Cristaidi*. We eventually heard the story from Albinus, a monk who felt overwhelmed with guilt when he thought you had been drowned. You see, the *Cristaidi* sent you to Letha in a boat to have you tutored at a *Cristaidi* school. They wanted to keep you from our Druid teachings and tribal ways, and planned to have you raised as a Roman *Cristaide* and then bring you back to the island and set you on the throne. With your bloodlines and birthright, you would be a powerful force against us. They wanted to strengthen their hold on the people, to convert them to their own god, Ísu."

Ethne continued the tale. "You were kidnapped and taken to sea as planned, but a storm came up and the boat was lost; that much we knew, but no more. My heart was broken when they took you, and I could no longer handle the complaints of the *Cristaidi* and the warriors. Cadla gathered a large faction around him, and there was an election. He won, and I left for the forest, thinking only of keeping the Druid ways alive as the new religion swept through the *flaith* and the common people."

Lucius was silent for a long while, gazing into the embers of the hearth. He thought of Abbott Mihael, whom he had loved as a father. Was it possible for the abbott to betray him like that? He felt a searing pain, remembering all the lonely years when he had lain on his cot, longing for a family to call his own. Forgiveness followed. Druid-trained, he knew how to move his emotions to his third eye to achieve *sith*.

"I can see the pattern of their thoughts. It was a logical plan, but brutal for a small boy. And it was a terrible thing to do to you, Mother." His voice cracked with emotion.

Ruadh put his hand on Lucius's shoulder. "How is it that you are here and under guard?"

"I came here from Innis nan Druidneach with my love, whom I intend to handfast. She wanted me to meet Gaine and the both of you. She said you were her teachers. Her name is Aífe," he added.

"Aífe!" Ethne cried with delight. "She is as a daughter to us! We sent her to the Druid Isle to learn the finer arts of *filidecht*. How in all the worlds did *you* end up there?"

Lucius told them of his strange travels, of his long search to find his blood-kin, and of the intervention of the gods.

"You have made a great *imramm*, my son," said Ruadh. "One worthy of legend and song. But where is Aífe now?"

"She went with the funeral procession to bury Gaine. We were with Gaine when she passed over, and then Martinus and his monks appeared with orders to keep me under guard. I never had a chance to explain to her what happened. She expected me to be there for the funeral. She must be very worried."

"They will be back in a few days. That will give us time to talk and catch up and plan your handfasting," Ethne said, already thinking of a traditional full moon rite in the circle of stones outside of the *rath*, just as she had performed with Ruadh so many sun-cycles before. The memory of it brought a smile to her face and a joy that she had not felt in many turnings of the seasons. Ruadh caught her expression and knew exactly what she was thinking. He reached for her hand and squeezed it, his eyes twinkling a little as he gazed on her happy face.

45

Cadla's rough treatment of Aífe caused concern among the *flaith*. Since she did not complain or cry out, everyone assumed she had accepted the role of concubine. It was not uncommon for a woman to take such a position, especially at Lugnasad, when contracts for the job were written up by the Brehons. A woman could agree to be a concubine for one turning of the sun or sign on for a lifetime. But the young woman was strangely silent, and as the days passed, dark circles grew under her eyes.

Since Aífe no longer resisted, Cadla bullied her more, openly insulting her by slapping her bottom at the feast while everyone watched. He enjoyed these petty acts of humiliation, thinking they were a just reward for her earlier disrespect.

The women of the *flaith* were scandalized; a royal concubine might bear a child who would be as eligible for the throne as any prince of the blood and deserved more respect than this. With the intuition of women, they pieced together that Cadla was punishing the beautiful woman for scorning him. But they could not fathom why she stayed mute; this was not the usual behavior of a woman of the tribes.

"He must have some mysterious hold over her," one said.

"If I were her, I'd claw his eyes out," said another.

"I think she is just getting what she deserves, for her pride in rejecting him last spring," sniffed a recent convert to the *Cristaidi* faith.

By the time the funeral procession neared the *rath* once more, the *flaith* and the villagers were divided into firm factions on the subject. Some supported Aífe in her plight, and others felt the Ard-Rí had every right to control her as he wished. The latter faction was mostly *Cristaidi*; those who adhered to the old religion were of the former frame of mind.

Ethne, Ruadh, and Lucius had told their story to the warriors, workers, and clergy who had remained behind in the *rath*, and everyone except Tanaide and Eógan had listened respectfully. The princes were quick to grasp that Lucius, now called Prince Ruadhán, was a threat to both of them. If he succeeded in persuading the tribes that he was the son of the old Ard-Rí and Ard-Rígain, he could compete for the throne. Tanaide and Eógan wanted no one else to believe he was thus entitled.

Martinus felt powerless in the face of Ruadh and Ethne's rescue of Lucius. If he could have, he would have simply had them killed. But Ruadh and Ruadhán were always wary, sword at the ready, and Ethne never walked anywhere without a dirk in her belt and another in her boot. To make matters worse, they had been roaming the *tuath*, telling their tale to anyone who would listen. It was fast becoming the most exciting news of the day.

They would not go quietly, that was certain. And the memories of the reign of Crimthann and Ethne were still strong with the people. They would be outraged if anything happened to Ethne or her husband. Their deaths would bring certain chaos to In Medon.

Besides, their son had been raised by the brothers at Inissi Leuca. Perhaps he would still make a *Cristaide* king. There might yet be a way to twist these events to favor the true religion.

Everyone waited tensely for the Ard-Rí's return.

"It can't be!" the old Abbott Germanus said, rubbing his eyes. He had come upon Ethne, Ruadh, and Ruadhán as they walked under the apple trees outside of the gates. He thought he must be seeing things, or perhaps his mind was finally breaking under the strain of age. He reached out to touch Lucius, now called Ruadhán, and see if he was real or simply a vision.

"Crimthann?" the old abbott inquired softly, with a look of wonder.

"No, sir, I am not he. I am his son."

Germanus had been absent from the *rath* for a few days because his joints and bones had hurt too much to brave the out-of-doors, but the old man remembered clearly the schemes that he and Albinus had set in play so many sun-tides before. It seemed to him that God had fulfilled yet another of his grand designs and brought the now-*Cristaide* prince back to take the throne. Even better, his Drui mother, that bothersome old queen, actually seemed happy for once. Everything was finally going according to plan.

"*Deo gratias*," he murmured piously as his eyes looked the handsome prince up and down. But he wondered why the prince was dressed as a Drui. Perhaps it was a disguise. It was a mystery still to be unraveled.

"Are you actually grateful for our son's safe return?" asked Ruadh sarcastically.

"Of course, of course I am," Germanus said in an oily tone. He suspected that the young man's parents must not be aware of the master plan after all. He would have to speak with the prince in private and ferret out how much he knew about the great destiny that had been set for him since infancy. All in due time.

"Prince Ruadhán, I will champion you with the *flaith* and the people, should you decide to seek the throne," Germanus added quickly, wanting to firmly cement his ties with the intended future Ard-Ri.

An unspoken look flashed between Ethne, Ruadh, and the prince, who had already worked out a plan of their own.

After supper, when most had retired for the day, the old abbott found an excuse to separate the prince from his parents and bid him come to examine the construction site.

"What do you think? Is it up to the standards of Inissi Leuca, my son?"

"I suppose so, though it is rather smaller than the chapel there."

"We do what we can with what we are given to work with, you know," the abbott replied. "We're acting in haste because we want the foundation to be firmly laid before the Ard-Ri and the others get back. We don't want anyone to reverse our plans.

"Now we're in need of a strong *Cristaide* leader to pull the tribes together and steer them on the right path. You are trained for the priesthood and are a prince of the royal line. Who is there better than you to take up this task? You are the perfect candidate to complete our mission."

Ruadhán noticed that the man was clutching his hands unconsciously, as if he were grasping for something priceless, just beyond reach.

To the abbott's pleasure, Ruadhán assented.

"I am trained in the ways of Inissi Leuca, and I understand your wishes. But it will be many years yet before Cadla is ready to step down."

"Don't you worry about that. All things are possible in the eyes of the Lord."

The abbott went off to find Martinus, Isidore, and Teilo and bring them the good news.

46

There was to be a feast that evening in honor of the *flaith* who had accompanied the Ard-Ri on his processional and to celebrate the clearing of the *nemed* and the laying of the foundation for the new chapel. The news of Lucius's arrival had whipped through the people like a windstorm, and Cadla decided to downplay the event by acting unconcerned. He did not want to enhance Ethne, Ruadh, or Ruadhán's status by publicly acknowledging them, but privately he was worried. He would have to do everything in his power to secure his own image before the *flaith*.

"You will wear the finest silks tonight. It will be a credit to me," Cadla ordered Aífe. His dead wife's wooden chest was still full of gowns, capes, and jewels.

"Pick something from Nárbflaith's clothes box. She was far more beautiful than you, but her clothes will make you appear worthy in the eyes of the court."

His petty humiliations no longer fazed her. He was utterly transparent. He was clearly afraid of her, else why would he try so hard to keep her in her place? As she bathed and dressed for the evening, her thoughts were with Lucius, thinking that surely, surely he would come for her now, or that she would soon receive a message.

The Great Hall was hung with garlands of new wheat and scarlet field poppies in honor of the season. Freshly cut rushes lay scattered on the floors, and the wolf hounds that lurked under the tables to clean up fallen scraps had been carefully washed and combed. Huge loaves of oat bread made from new grain graced the center of the high table, interspersed with wooden vats of freshly churned butter, beeswax candles in intricately wrought iron holders, and small bronze containers of salt. Freshly cleaned woven cloths on the walls provided a riot of color, and the carvings of interlaced animals and plants that graced the room partitions and the large panel behind the throne had been polished until they gleamed.

An entire ox was slaughtered and roasted for the *flaith* and the warriors, and several sheep and a quantity of chickens were roasted to be distributed to any of the lower classes who hung around the gates. Meat, bread, and ale would also be sent to the revelers attending the Lugnasad fires that dotted the nearby hilltops. Cadla was ever mindful of his reputation, knowing that to be hospitable was the surest route to continued power.

He gave final instructions to Aífe in the privacy of his chamber. "You will act as my hostess tonight, and since it is an official feast, there will be a formal distribution of liquor to the warriors and the *flaith*. You will pass the cup to me first as the highest-ranking person in the hall, then to the man on my right, Máel Ísu, then to the man on my left. After that, you will fill two bowls to be passed down each side of the table. Everyone will drink in order of precedence, and each will speak a sacred oath over the bowl as they hold it. Do you understand?"

Aífe nodded. She knew she would be distracted—the first thing she would want to do once she entered the hall would be to look for Lucius—but she would have to concentrate carefully on her appointed duty. The passing of a formal bowl of liquor at the feast was a sacred function, and she would be royal consort, hostess, and priestess at once, a serious task.

Warriors had been known to kill each other if the bowl of liquor was handed to them out of order or if they perceived an insult to their rank, and any oath that was sworn out loud over liquor at the feast had to be fulfilled or the speaker be willing to die in the effort. With all the peers of the realm as witness, it was nearly impossible to undo an oath once it was uttered over the ritual cup. The image of the last official caup Cadla had passed to her at a feast still burned within her heart. She used all her Druid discipline to will away the memory.

At last, everything was ready. Huge torches were lit and stuck into the iron sconces that projected from the stout timbers of the walls and from the roof trees. The great central hearth was ablaze; an enormous cauldron of spiced cider simmered on the fire to lend a sweet scent to the room and to provide liquid refreshment.

One by one, the *flaith* entered and were led to their seats, each one gorgeously dressed in bright colors and jealously guarding their privilege by sitting as near the throne as possible. Each noble who sat at the table had a warrior standing behind him, fully armed and ready to defend to the death the nobleman to whom he was assigned, most often a member of his own kin-group. The women, adorned in their most colorful tunics, best jewels, and elaborate hair braids, sat in rows against the back walls. The air reeked of competition and jealousy.

Cadla entered the hall followed by Aífe, keeping a pace or two behind, as she had been instructed. She used all of her will to keep her awareness in the objectivity of her third eye, as she had been taught in the lesson of *súil inmedónach*, forging a mask of tranquility on her face as she scanned the hall for Lucius. Where was he? Forbidden to speak, she could not even ask for him, lest she receive another welt or bruise. She hid past bruises and dark finger marks with a silken shawl.

Aífe's golden diadem gleamed in the firelight as she bent over a side table to fill the ritual cup and bowls. The orb on her head proclaimed that this was no ordinary feast but rather one with sacral overtones, a solemn occasion of state.

Máel Ísu, seated to the right of the throne, enjoyed the spectacle as if it were his own personal triumph and proudly stood to open the proceedings with a prayer as but a short time before it would have been the role of a Drui to do:

Brethren, be joyful.
Now that you have been set free from sin
And you have been made slaves of the one true God
You will get a reward leading to your sanctification
And ending in eternal life in heaven.
Thanks be to the one true God for this glorious food
  and this splendid company.
And thanks be to the one true God for our new church. Amen.

He sat, and Cadla rose to address the gathering. "Welcome, my friends and relations. The sacred drink that we are about to partake of is a symbol of my esteem for you all. Aífe will act in the stead of my beloved Nárbflaith, who should have been the one to officiate at this meal. The cup that Aífe will pass is filled with *fíon*, a substitute for blood. It symbolizes the red blood of kinship and the mystical blood bond that you as the *flaith* of In Medon share with me and my sons. We are all one family here.

"As each of us takes a sip, let us remember our sacred duty to uphold and defend each other, just as if we were blood-kin. Let each of you utter a sacred oath over your cup in the hearing of your wives. For two things encourage a warrior best: when the family fights together, and when women are witness to a warrior's actions." Cadla smiled graciously towards the ranks of women seated against the walls.

The air in the room grew thicker. The business of making a sacred oath was often a deadly one, with many unforeseen turnings.

Suddenly, a cold wind gusted from the direction of the door. Torches guttered as everyone craned their necks to see what had caused the disturbance. Then a collective gasp escaped from every mouth.

Ethne, Ruadh, and Prince Ruadhán entered the hall dressed in gorgeous attire, thanks to the efforts of Abbott Germanus. Golden torcs glistened on their necks, and each wore a richly colored tunic covered by a six-colored cape, fastened with an enormous golden brooch.

Ethne's hair was carefully braided into intricate loops and whirls and woven through with golden ornaments. Ruadh and Ruadhán had golden armbands and long swords sheathed in scabbards of intricately worked red leather. Each had a beautifully polished bronze and silver shield strapped over his shoulder. It was a splendid entrance; there was no mistaking the royal rank of the three.

Most recognized Ethne and Ruadh, remembering them from years past. But none knew who the handsome young stranger at their side could possibly be.

The *flaith* waited for Cadla to change the order of precedence for seating; clearly the newcomers were of royal rank and deserved to sit at or very near the head of the table. But Cadla did not follow accepted protocol. Instead, he ordered the slaves to bring an extra bench and seat the three at the foot of the long line of guests.

A flurry of hushed whispers swept the hall. Why was the king making such a dangerous blunder?

"Silence!" Cadla roared, red-faced and flustered, aware that he had made a possibly fatal mistake but determined to diminish the status of his old rival. *How dare that woman show herself here now? This is a celebration of the triumph of all my plans and of the new religion. She has no business inserting herself just when that old witch Gaine is finally dead!* he thought in dismay.

"I am not impressed by your rich robes and gleaming jewels," he said. "Your day is long past. A new order rules in this kingdom, and there is no place left for *Pagani* like you. Your place is in the forest with outlaws and thieves, but I will allow you to sit at the very lowest end of the table."

The reference to outlaws and thieves was clearly aimed at Ruadh, and the mention of a new order was meant to insult Ethne and all the Druid, but the three at the foot of the table made no move to defend their honor. Their faces remained impassive, their tempers cool.

"Aífe, pass the cup now," Cadla commanded.

Aífe had watched the entrance of the three with fascination and relief. She knew that her liberation was finally at hand, and she was overjoyed to see her foster parents Ethne and Ruadh in the full splendor of their rank, but she could not fathom why Lucius should be with them and dressed in such finery. It was very strange to her eyes. At once, she recalled the vision she had of him dressed in princely garb. *He must wonder at me in these silks*, she thought. And yet the sight of him was like feeling the warm breeze of Innis nan Druidneach blowing softly across the summer sands.

Cadla's words still echoed in her ears. She remembered his stern instructions to pass the cup first to the highest-ranking person in the hall. If Cadla could insult *Pagani* of royal rank by seating them at the foot of the table, well, she would right the wrong by turning the insult on its head. As priestess and cup-bearer, it was her choice how to order the cup offering. She recalled the lesson of *commus*, learned at such a cost on the cliff face of Innis nan Druidneach. Suddenly the candles around her glowed like the yellow citrine in her crane bag, carefully hidden under her gown.

She walked to the foot of the table amidst the shocked whispers of the dinner guests and solemnly handed the ritual cup to Ruadh. But Ruadh refused it with a hand gesture and graciously offered it to Ethne. Ethne also refused it politely and handed it to Ruadhán, who accepted it with a bow of his head and a smile.

"I will accept this cup from your hand, lady," he said, addressing Ethne but looking into Aífe's eyes.

As he spoke, the warriors drew their swords and the *flaith* pulled out their dirks, prepared to avenge the deadly insult to the Ard-Rí.

"Friends, lay down your weapons," Ruadhán said in an even tone, rising slowly from his seat. "Do you not know who I am?"

The hall went silent as the black door of midnight. Everyone waited for an explanation.

"Germanus, tell them." Ruadhán looked in the direction of the old man sitting in the shadows, gumming a piece of soft bread. Germanus cleared his throat, spat on the floor, and rose, leaning heavily on his stick.

"This young man is the son of the Ard-Rí Crimthann and of the Ard-Rígain Ethne, who sits here at the bottom of the table. Cadla did wrong to put them at the foot of the table, and he knows it. Prince Ruadhán is a trained *Cristaide* brother who would have been a priest, except he has returned to rule In Medon." The old man sat down, gloating toothlessly.

"I have something to say too," Aífe quickly interjected, pitching her voice of authority to ensure everyone's attention. She bared her arms and revealed the bruises and marks of Cadla's fingers.

"This is the work of the Ard-Ri. I did not cry out until now because he threatened to kill me if I did, and I could think of no one who would come to my defense."

Ruadhán let out a roar and moved to charge Cadla, but Ethne threw her arm forcefully against his chest. She would not lose her son again, not now and not in this way.

"The shame!" Ethne cried out, seeing Aífe's bruises.

"This is not the behavior of a just king!" Ruadh exclaimed.

Cadla knew instantly that this blight on his character would cost him the throne. He rose from his seat so quickly that it was knocked over. "You bitch!" he cried. With nothing left to lose, he unsheathed his sword and charged at Aífe, his weapon aiming for her heart. But he was blinded by rage, and Ruadh was quicker and more focused. As Ruadh lunged forward, Cadla stumbled, toppled, and fell onto his blade.

The guests sat, frozen. To avenge the dying Ard-Ri would place them on the wrong side of Prince Ruadhán. No one was willing to take that risk save Tanaide and Eógan, who pulled their swords from their sheaths, preparing to defend their wounded parent. But with no one to help them they slowly backed down, watching helplessly as their father's life-blood seeped into the rushes.

"It is the will of God," Máel Ísu pronounced as he knelt over Cadla to administer the last rites.

The crowd in the hall waited in horrified silence until Ruadhán raised the ritual cup and intoned an oath so that all could hear. "I vow to hold an election for the position of Ard-Ri, and I vow to handfast Aífe, the woman I love."

He took the ritual sip and solemnly passed the cup to Ethne, who vowed to defend and protect her son and Aífe to her dying breath. Then Ruadh pledged an oath to give his right arm, his battle experience, and all the strength of the *fiana* to the prince.

The cup was passed from the bottom of the table to the top, and no one objected, so amazed were they by the events of the evening and so grateful that they would not have to fight and die for Cadla's honor.

47

R uadh took a small retinue of warriors and visited each of the minor kingdoms of In Medon in turn, making sure that each petty king and queen understood the true story of Ruadhán's parentage and assuring them that the might of the *fiana* would be behind the prince, should he ascend the throne. He emphasized Ruadhán's *Cristaide* education and his training at Innis nan Druidneach as a *fili*, a status that made the prince uniquely qualified to serve and protect both religions.

"In the past, we had warrior-kings who were served by a Drui. Now we will have a Drui king who will be served by warriors," he told the nobles, emphasizing the strength of the young prince, whom he knew was no battle leader.

Meanwhile, Ethne met with the Druid of the smaller kingdoms to ensure that they would lobby the kings and queens they served to back the prince in the coming election. She knew that Ruadhán already had the support of the *Cristaidi*, thanks to Germanus.

The building of the stone chapel continued under Máel Ísu's watchful eye, while Ruadhán and Aífe supervised the reconstruction of the ancient holy well near the *rath* that had been sorely neglected during the years of *Cristaidi* dominance. The well was overgrown with weeds and the waters had silted up, but the path to it was well worn by the feet of the devout *Pagani* who still came to offer their coins to the waters and hang their prayer cloths on a nearby hawthorn tree.

Ruadhán and Aífe reconsecrated the well in the name of the fire goddess Brighid: "For where fire and water come together, there is the greatest potential for magic," as Bébinn and Amalgáid had taught.

They hung their own strips of prayer cloth on the ancient hawthorn overhanging the well, making a public show of support for the *Pagani* who came to make similar devotions, and washed the large stone near the well with milk, honey, and the Waters of Life, to honor its spirit and reawaken its powers to bless the land.

The people wondered how these Druid of the highest rank, trained in the arts of *filidecht*, could be so tolerant of the *Cristaide* church that was sprouting in the very heart of the old *nemed*.

"If there is one truth that the art of *filidecht* has shown us, it is that all paths to the divine are sacred, as are all lives and beings on the face of the land, sea, and sky," said Ruadhán.

"We have no quarrel with the teachings of the god Ísu, though we dislike the way some of his followers impose their religion on the people, as if theirs were the only way. All the gods should be honored and respected, for that is the way of *sith*."

He thought of Martinus, who had left in haste before the banquet with Isidore and Teilo the moment he received word that he was officially named bishop by the pope.

"The so-called disciples of Ísu like Martinus and his followers, who are already back in Letha desecrating trees, wells, shrines, and stones that others hold sacred, are misguided. Their vision is clouded because they do not respect the whole of creation. Their way leads to terrible destruction and sorrow." Ruadhán raised his *cristall glain* to the sun and watched as rainbows of color spread on the grass like many paths and ways streaming from the one pure Source, reminding him of the lesson of *solus* from Innis nan Druidneach.

Ever after, the folk would use such stones for magical healing work after imbuing them with sunlight and moonlight to waken their powers.

Cináed of Irardacht and Rochad of Torcrad, high kings of the northern and southern kingdoms, sensed a weakness in the prince, given his youth and lack of battle testing. They prepared for the upcoming election by camping outside of the *rath* with their warriors and tribal leaders, each on opposite sides of the main gate. They staged daily battle contests and competitions with swords and arrows before the *dun* to remind the people of their warrior skills and distributed food and drink to the spectators, hoping to impress them with their generosity.

Both sent emissaries to the smaller kingdoms of In Medon bearing gifts, hoping to strengthen their claims to the high throne with gold. The position of Ard-Ri of the central kingdom of In Medon was the highest honor the island had to offer, and both men had waited most of their lives for such a chance.

Daire, the eldest son of Crimthann, received an emissary sent by Ethne and Ruadh to the Forest School but had no thought of standing as a candidate. The ways of the court were not a pleasant memory for him after his father's shocking death from a poisoned blade, and he preferred to stay in the forest with the students. He knew he was more a Drui than a politician. The task of passing on the Druid ways from one generation to the next were as sacred to him as any throne, and so he sent the messenger back with assurances that he would not challenge Ruadhán at present or at any time in the future.

On the full moon of Cantlos, Aífe and Ruadhán were handfasted at the newly refurbished holy well, where they passed a silver chalice of pure water to each other and went naked into the waters to be twice born in the sight of Ethne, Ruadh, and the Druid. The *Cristaidi* priests stayed away, appalled that the prince and princess had chosen a *Pagani* ceremony to mark their union.

That same night, Ruadhán led Aífe to the ancient stone circle on the hill outside of the *rath,* where they consummated their union in a private ceremony on a flaming red blanket under the stars.

When the election was finally held, it was quickly apparent that Cináed and Rochad had miscalculated the power and influence that the Druid and the *fiana* still held. They had thought that their gifts of gold and promises of strength in battle would be enough to secure their status in the eyes of the kingdoms. But the reasoned words of Ethne and Ruadh had carried more weight, as had the revered memory of Gaine, Coemgen, Crimthann, and all the glories of the past to which Ruadhán seemed heir.

There was no thought of a horse sacrifice to seal Ruadhán's Marriage to the Land. In the old days, the new king would have mated with a sacred mare and then bathed in her broth and eaten of her flesh, but this rite was too offensive to *Cristaidi* sensibilities. Instead, the old custom was revived of staging a horse race around the hill of the ancient stone circle. There was a massive fair, a poetry competition, and tests of athletic and warrior skill on the grassy lawn between the hill and the *rath*. Aífe handed out every prize with her own hands.

"She looks like the Land Goddess herself, bestowing her favors," Ethne commented.

There was feasting and *mid* for everyone in the kingdom for three nights and days.

As one of their first tasks of leadership, Ruadhán and Aífe made sure that the Forest School was well endowed to flourish in the wilderness for centuries.

"It is ever the way of the world for there to be conflict, but there must always be those who keep the dream of peace alive: peace between peoples, kingdoms, and religions," said Ruadhán, cradling his wife in his arms under the light of a full moon, beneath silvered trees.

"And our love must always be larger than just our love for each other," Aífe added. "We must be good stewards of this kingdom, but the love and care of all creatures, plants, animals, and people is our true mission and the message that we must repeat at every chance. This is the flame that we must pass along to the Druid of the future."

"Does this mean that the *fili* have fully accepted the new *Cristaide* religion?" Ruadh asked Ethne some time later, as they sat before their own hearth-fire at the Forest School.

"For now they have," Ethne replied. "But the nature of the world is change, and we must be ready for the winds that blow from many quarters. Our task is to keep the old ways alive for the future—a precious treasure never to be lost and ready to be taken up again whenever it is needed."

"Untruth yields to truth."
—A maxim from *Audacht Morainn,*
an ancient Irish wisdom text

epiLogue

Oruid instruction on Innis nan Druidneach continued for several generations more, until the sacred island of the Druids was taken over by Christian missionaries in the fifth century CE. Today the old magic is once again returning to its shores.

Historical Note

*T*he story you just read came from my own *imbas* (poetic imagination) and is not based on historical characters; however, Innis nan Druidneach is a real place in the Hebrides of Scotland that was once a sacred island of the Druids. The shores of Northern Ireland are but a short sail away from its southern beach.

I am grateful to members of the Findhorn Community for telling me of the power spots inherent in the island's landscape. I spent an entire week searching them out for myself in the summer of 1983.

In the very early medieval period, the *fili* of Ireland made a peaceful and seamless transition to the Celtic Christian church, becoming clergy in the new faith, whose early beliefs were a mixture of the ancient Celtic reverence for nature and biblical philosophy. The character of the native Celtic church was changed dramatically when it eventually came under the dominance of Rome and its link with ancient Celtic beliefs and practices was officially severed.

The Celtic Christian church is currently enjoying a revival in Ireland and Britain, where the reverence for holy wells, fire, water, and trees was never completely lost, while Druidism and Celtic Reconstructionist Paganism are part of the current Pagan revival, one of the fastest-growing religious movements in the world today.

As the old saying goes, "Scratch the surface of a good Irish Catholic, and underneath you will find a Pagan."

Notes

1. The Romano-Gaulish Coligny calendar as interpreted by Monard (1999) and others:

Samonios (Oct/Nov): "seed fall" (Samain)

Dvmann[osios] (Nov/Dec): "dark month"

Rivros (Dec/Jan): "frost month"

Anagantio[s] (Jan/Feb): "stay at home"

Ogronios (Feb/Mar): "ice month"

Cvtios (Mar/Apr): "shower of rain," also Sonnocingos, "beginning of spring," "wind month"

Giamonios (Apr/May): "shoots month" (Beltaine)

Simivisonios (May/Jun): "mid spring," "bright month"

Eqvos (Jun/Jul): "horse month," "time of the herds"

Elembiv[ios] (Jul/Aug): "stag month," "claim time" (Lugnasad)

Aedrinios (Aug/Sep): "hot month" (*aed* is "fire"), "arbitration time"

Cantlos (Sep/Oct): "song month" (harvest)

Each month of the calendar is divided into a dark half and a light half, and each day is designated as *Mat(os)*, "lucky," or *Anm(atos)*, "unlucky." There are symbols on the calendar for Beltaine (Giamonios Full Moon), Lugnasad (Elembivios Full Moon) and Samain (Samonios Full Moon). The inscription *Trinvx[tion] Samo[nii] Sindiv* ("three nights of Samonios today") implies that Samonios was a three-day festival. There is no designation for Imbolc, which may be a more northern (Irish) holy day.

2. Based on the poem *"Acallam na Senórach"* (The Colloquy of the Ancients), a late twelfth-century monastic compilation that includes traditional Celtic rules of behavior, in which Finn gives advice on how to behave as a gentleman.

3. This song is loosely based on a poem about the coming of the sons of Míl to Ireland by the bard Amairgen Glúingeal, as given in a translation by R. A. S. Macalister (ed.) in *Lebor Gabála Érenn* (V, 110–113). In the Hindu Bhagavad-Gita ("Song of God"), Sri Krishna sings a similar lay: "I am the radiant sun...I am the moon...I am Meru of the mountain peaks..."

Postscript to Ellen Evert Hopman's *The Druid Isle*, otherwise known as:

what's that doing in there?

by Shambhala Nath (Donald Michael Kraig)

In the novel you have just enjoyed, beginning in chapter twenty-nine, Bébinn begins instructing Aífe in *ecnae nathairech*, or serpent wisdom. For those who have studied even a little bit of spiritual lore, it is obvious that this wisdom is very similar to the Eastern concepts of kundalini and the chakras. While some might condemn this as a form of questionable or even illegitimate cross-cultural contamination of dubious historicity, wondering *what's that doing in there*, I'm not so sure. To understand why, I'd like to take you back several thousand years.

The word *Hindu* is not based on anything religious, it is simply based on location. Specifically, it is derived from the Sanskrit word *sindhu*, meaning "river," and it specifically refers to the Indus River, a geological divide at the northwest of the Indian subcontinent. It was first used to refer to India as a subcontinent in the mid-seventeenth century. It wasn't used to represent the religions of India until 1829. The actual name for the religion we call "Hinduism" today is *Sanatana Dharma*, a Sanskrit phrase meaning "the eternal law."

As you may know, the holy river of Hinduism is the Ganga (Ganges). What you may not know is that before the Ganga became such a focus, there was another river in the area, the Saraswati, which was considered the sacred river. And around it was an entire culture, the Harappan culture, which predated the India of today. At its height, one of the cities of this culture, Mohenjo-daro, had a population that was larger than the combined population of the Northern and Southern Kingdoms of Egypt. It was a highly advanced country, with trade going all over and living in peace. So why don't you know about it?

There are a couple of reasons. First, many of the archeological sites are in Kashmir, and that land, unfortunately, is a hotbed of violence, making excavations difficult. The second major reason is one man, Max Müller (1823–1900).

Müller was a linguist working in India and sponsored by the British. He noticed something that others had noticed but that really bothered him. Sanskrit, the language of ancient India, had many words that were similar to much later words found in European languages. Since Sanskrit came earlier, it must be assumed that those Sanskrit words were the source of the European words. But Sanskrit was the language of the dark-skinned people of India. How could they have produced an advanced culture? Unfortunately, Müller was a racist. And he had a solution.

Without any training or physical research in archeology, Müller formulated the theory that a light-skinned race of people known as the "Aryans" from Europe invaded India, bringing civilization. He even gave a date for this "invasion." He claimed it happened around 1500 BCE. It must have happened around then, according to him, because he also happened to believe in the religious teachings of archbishop James Ussher, who came to the conclusion that God created the world on the night before October 23, 4004 BCE, and around 2448 BCE was the date of Noah's ark. So this invasion, now known as the Aryan invasion, must have occurred later.

Unfortunately, there are some major problems with this theory. There's no archeological evidence that such an invasion ever occurred. There's no literature from these "advanced" Aryans, while there is lots of literature from the supposedly unadvanced dark-skinned Indians. Modern DNA research shows there was never such an invasion. Even the Sanskrit word *Aryan* only means "noble" or "honorable," and referred to a class of people, not some mythical "race."

And yet, the idea of an Aryan invasion was accepted. There were a few reasons for that. First, the British liked the idea of telling a people they subjugated that, historically, a foreign, light-skinned race had brought civilization to India. They felt it would make the local population easier to control, so they supported the idea. Some German theologians and mystics liked the idea also, because they didn't want to trace Western civilization back to the Middle East and especially to Jewish culture. There is even a belief that the mythical Aryan race came from Atlantis. Thus, in support of politics, religion, mysticism, racism, and anti-Semitism, a theory was created that is still taught in many schools today.

Actual history and archeology shows an advanced local culture. So what happened to the Harappans? The Saraswati River, upon which they depended, dried up. I am told there is a myth about this. The goddess Saraswati was being too noisy, so she was told to be quiet. She did so by vanishing underground. By around 2000 BCE, with the river that had been its focus gone, the mighty Harappan culture vanished.

Where did they go? Evidence seems to indicate that many slowly moved from northwest of India into the subcontinent. Others moved northeast to Tibet and China. However, others moved further west, all the way to Europe.

Is there any evidence to support this? Besides the language, there is a very famous item found in Denmark in 1891 that dates from the first or second century BCE known as the Gundestrup Cauldron. On it are figures that clearly are derived from India and show Indian deities and elephants. One of the most interesting figures is that of a man wearing horns and sitting in a cross-legged position. At a Mohenjo-daro excavation, a seal was found showing a form of the deity Shiva, Pashupati, the Lord of Animals. It is virtually the same as that on the Gundestrup Cauldron. Both look remarkably like descriptions of Cernnunos.

So there is both linguistic evidence and archeological evidence of a connection between that ancient people of India and the Celts. There is also some remarkable evidence in what we know of the Druids, the spiritual leaders of the Celtic people, that links them to ancient India. According to some authorities, the Druids claimed to be descended from the original children or tribe of Danu, the Tuatha de Danaan. The worship of the goddess Danu seems to have existed all over the ancient Celtic world, as evidenced in the names of rivers such as the Danube River in Germany, the Don and Dneiper Rivers in Russia, etc. Well, it so happens that Danu is also an early Hindu Goddess, physically of the primeval waters and astrologically of the Milky Way. In what many consider to be the oldest Sanskrit text, the Rig Veda, she is clearly called the mother of a tribe known as the Danavas, or children of Danu. The Druidic teachings on reincarnation, justice, consciousness, and an inner spiritual light are amazingly similar to ancient Indic beliefs. It is certainly possible that all of these similarities are nothing more than coincidence, but with so many links I find it highly unlikely.

But what about the ancient beliefs from India as they relate to the book you have just read? To truly understand what the power centers are from an ancient viewpoint, we need to look at the way the mind works and its interrelationship with the body.

Of course, we have physical bodies, but that's obvious. What is it that animates the body? That must be some sort of energy. What controls the body and the energy? The mind. What makes a superior mind? Knowledge and wisdom. And what do you get from knowledge and wisdom? Pure spiritual bliss. Now, if we have a physical body, couldn't we conceive of these other qualities as non-physical bodies? Indeed, that's exactly what is done. And these five bodies, or sheaths (Sanskrit: *koshas*), make up the totality of who we are.

Within those sheaths are pathways of energy. There are literally dozens of such pathways. The concept of these energy pathways is at the root of ancient Indian medical practices (Ayurveda) and was carried into China, where they are now known as meridians. Where the paths cross are centers of power, often seen as spinning disks by people with spiritual vision. They are known as chakras (the "ch" is pronounced hard, as in "chalk," or even like a hard "k," but never soft, as if it were spelled "shakras"). There are literally hundreds of them throughout our bodies. (No, they are not the basis of the acupuncture points. Those are based on the crossings of three energy paths, and the points are called marmas.)

Of course, some chakras are more important than others. According to the earliest descriptions, there were only three that were important: one associated with the genitals, one with the heart, and one at the crown of the head. The chakras allow for a flow of energy between the sheaths of our bodies. In a sense, they are spiritual counterparts to the neurotransmitters that send information from neurons to each cell of the body. Each chakra is a vortex that allows information and energy to flow between the sheaths and outside. Each has its own functions such as are described in the novel.

Today, the most common description of the major chakras is that there are seven. Although they are not physical themselves, they are associated with the tip of the tailbone, the sexual organs, the solar plexus, the heart, the throat, the brow, and the top of the head. Some people don't count the uppermost chakra, as its functions are so completely different than the lower six, so they describe only six major chakras.

Other schools describe different numbers of chakras. For example, what is arguably the most sacred symbol in India is the Sri Yantra. It is composed of nine intersecting triangles surrounded by rings of circles, metaphoric lotus petals, and an outer "square" which has outcroppings on each side. For those of you who are familiar with it, the Sri Yantra has some similarities to the Kabalistic Tree of Life. However, it is far more, with some people who study the knowledge of the Sri Yantra (Sri Vidya) actually worshipping the diagram. Some followers of Sri Vidya work with a nine-chakra system. The last two are more ethereal than the usual seven. They are found within the head and are sometimes said to be two parts of one chakra.

The serpent energy described in this novel matches the concept of the ancient Indian energy known as the kundalini, which is described as a serpent. The pathways for this energy in early illustrations show it merely going up the sides and center of the major chakras. Later, although the central path of the energy remains straight, the paths on the side (related to solar and lunar currents of energy) are shown to move from one side of the central path to the other, transitioning at the chakras.

Thus, the chakras are not only centers of moving energy (through the sheaths or bodies of the individual), but if they are blocked by excess or too little energy (or from problems with each of the sheaths—for example, with restricting thoughts in the mental sheath), the kundalini energy is blocked.

Through training and using various techniques ranging from visualization and breathwork to some of the sexual practices of Tantrics, the blockages can be freed, allowing the energy to flow. When all of the chakras are open and the energy flows freely, a person achieves a state of enlightenment.

Unlike just feeling good or feeling at one with the universe, this ancient freeing of personal and universal power is not simply a mental attitude. Since all of the sheaths are involved, the result trickles to all of the bodies, including the physical. Although some of the results are supposed powers, or *siddhis* (which may be metaphorical), there is one way to be sure you have achieved a state of enlightenment. When everything is working properly, the crown chakra inverts and pours a substance over the body known as amrita.[1] Amrita has an oily feel to it, so it is as if someone is pouring a pleasant, warm oil over your body. The body responds by actually changing the chemical structure of your liquid secretions. All of them, if tasted, become sweet to the taste. Even the saltiness of tears and perspiration become sweet. It is an amazing experience.

It would be impossible to describe all of the aspects of the chakras, koshas, kundalini, and more in just a brief postscript to this novel.

---

1   Today, there is group of people that identifies amrita with female sexual ejaculation. This is a new definition and does not equate with the traditional concept. That doesn't make it wrong, just different.

What I want to point out is that finding descriptions of the chakras and kundalini among the Druids is neither surprising nor out of place. Nor is finding systems of chakras with more or less than seven unusual. I would hope that this novel has done more than entertain. I hope that it also inspires you to seek even more information.

I would like to end this with the ancient word of greeting and parting that is still used in India today: *Namaste!* (That which is of the gods in me recognizes and acknowledges that which is of the gods in you.)

Some Sources:

Feuerstein, Georg, Subhash Kak, and David Frawley. *In Search of the Cradle of Civilization.* Wheaton, IL: The Theosophical Publishing House, 2001.

Rajaram, N. S. *Sarasvati River and the Vedic Civilization.* New Delhi: Aditya Prakashan, 2006.

Venugopalan, R. *Soul Searchers: The Hidden Mysteries of Kundalini.* New Delhi: B. Jain Publishers, 2002.

appeNᴆix 1
Christian Prayers

Prayer to Saint Michael the Archangel

Sancte Michael Archangele,
  defende nos in proelio, contra nequitiam
  et insidias diaboli esto praesidium.

Saint Michael the Archangel,
  defend us in battle;
  be our defense against the wickedness
  and snares of the devil.

Prayer for Protection

Exaudi nos, Domine sancte,
  Pater omnipotens, aeterne Deus,
  et mittere digneris sanctum Angelum tuum de coelis,
  qui custodiat, foveat,
  protegat, visitet atque defendat omnes habitants
  in hoc habitaculo.

Hear us, O holy Lord,
  almighty Father, everlasting God,
  and vouchsafe to send thy holy angel from heaven
  to guard, cherish, protect, visit, and defend all that are
  assembled in this place.

appenƌix 2
Further Reading

For a report on pollen studies that track the sudden
disappearance of yew in the early Christian period, see:

Molloy, K., and M. O'Connell. 2007. "Fresh insights into long-term
environmental change on the Aran Islands based on palaeo-eco-
logical investigations of lake sediments from Inis Oírr." *Journal
of the Galway Archaeological and Historical Society* 59:1–17.

For a discussion of trees in relation to late Iron Age ritual sites, see:

Newman, Connor, Michael O'Connell, Mary Dillon, and Karen
Molloy. 2007. "Interpretation of charcoal and pollen data relat-
ing to a late Iron Age ritual site in eastern Ireland: a holistic
approach." Published online 26 April 2006. *Vegetation History and
Archaeobotony* 16:349–365.

For a further understanding of Druid magic, Ogham, and the
spiritual and herbal uses of trees in the Celtic context, see:

Hopman, Ellen Evert. *A Druid's Herbal of Sacred Tree Medicine.*
Rochester, VT: Destiny Books, 2008.

For an overview of early Christian monastic life, see:

Campbell, Ewan. *Saints and Sea Kings.* Edinburgh: Canongate
Books, 1999.

Broun, Dauvit, and Owen Clancy Thomas, eds. *Spes Scotorum: Hope of Scots—Saint Columba, Iona and Scotland*. Edinburgh: T&T Clark, 1999.

For an overview of the ancient Brehon Laws, see:

Kelly, Fergus. *A Guide to Early Irish Law.* Dublin: Dublin Institute for Advanced Studies, 1991.

———. *Early Irish Farming*. Dublin: Dublin Institute for Advanced Studies, 1997.

———. *Bechbretha—An Old Irish Law-Tract on Bee-Keeping*. Dublin: Dublin Institute for Advanced Studies, 1983.

For an account of poetic training, the poetic grades, and laws pertaining to poets, see:

Breatnach, Liam, ed. *Uraichecht Na Riar*. Dublin: Dublin Institute for Advanced Studies, 1987.

For an example of a king-making ritual and the rules of good governance pertaining to ancient Irish kings, see:

Kelly, Fergus. *Audacht Morainn*. Dublin: Dublin Institute for Advanced Studies, 1976.

For background on the ritual use of intoxicating drinks from the La Téne to the Viking Age, see:

Enright, Michael J. *The Lady with a Mead Cup*. Dublin: Four Courts Press, 1996.

The Chakras

Information on the chakra systems is in part from class notes to Sri Yantra workshops given by Donald Michael Kraig and from Introduction to the Chakras, a class for the Grey School of Wizardry, by Donata Ahern, MSW, www.greyschool.com, as well as a lifetime of my own experience with various gurus and spiritual teachers.

Historical Resources

Chadwick, Nora. *The Celts.* Middlesex: Penguin, 1985.

Cunliffe, Barry. *The Celtic World: An Illustrated History of the Celtic Race, Their Culture, Customs and Legends.* New York: Greenwich House, 1986.

Green, Miranda. *The World of the Druids.* New York: Thames and Hudson, 1997.

Lincoln, Bruce. *Death, War and Sacrifice.* Chicago: University of Chicago Press, 1991.

Rees, Alwyn, and Brinley Rees. *Celtic Heritage, Ancient Tradition in Ireland and Wales.* New York: Thames and Hudson, 1994.

Ross, Anne. *Pagan Celtic Britain, Studies in Iconography and Tradition.* London: Routledge & Kegan Paul, 1967 (reprinted 1994).

Sjoestedt, Marie-Louise. *Gods and Heroes of the Ancient Celts.* New York: Dover Publications, 2000.

Wells, Peter. *Beyond Celts, Germans, and Scythians: Archaeology and Identity in Iron Age Europe.* London: Gerald Duckworth & Co., Ltd., 2002.

Aids to Creating Druid Rituals

Bord, Janet, and Colin Bord. *Earth Rites: Fertility Practices in Pre-Industrial Britain.* London: Granada Publishing Limited, 1983.

———. *Sacred Waters.* London: Paladin Grafton Books, 1986.

Carmichael, Alexander. *Carmina Gadelica: Hymns and Incantations.* Edinburgh: Floris Books, 1992.

Cross, Tom Peete, and Clark Harris Slover. *Ancient Irish Tales.* Totowa, NJ: Barnes and Noble Books, 1988 (reprint of the 1936 edition).

Hopman, Ellen Evert. *A Druid's Herbal for the Sacred Earth Year.* Rochester, VT: Destiny Books, 1995.

———. *A Druid's Herbal of Sacred Tree Medicine.* Rochester, VT: Destiny Books, 2008.

Kondratiev, Alexei. *Celtic Rituals: An Authentic Guide to Ancient Celtic Spirituality.* Scotland: New Celtic Publishing, 1999.

Information on Druids, Druid Orders, and Druid Training:

The Order of the Whiteoak (Ord na Darach Gile): www.whiteoakdruids.org

Ellen Evert Hopman's website: www.elleneverthopman.com

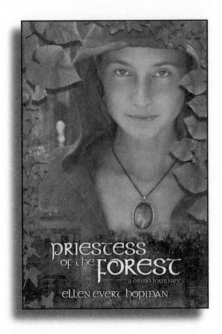

Priestess of the Forest
A Druid Journey

Ellen Evert Hopman

In the tradition of Marion Zimmer Bradley's *Mists of Avalon*, Ellen Evert Hopman weaves Druid history and spirituality into an engaging love story. This bardic teaching tale is set in fictional third-century Ireland when Christianity is sweeping across the Celtic Isles. During this time of crisis, love blooms between Ethne, a Druid healer, and her patient, a *fennid* warrior. Their passionate affair suffers a tragic blow when Ethne is called upon to become the high queen.

Told from the Druid perspective, Hopman re-creates the daily life, magical practices, politics, and spiritual lives of the ancient Celts during this historic turning point. Druid holy days, rites, rituals, herbal lore, and more are brought to life in this Celtic fantasy that illuminates Druidic teachings and cultural wisdom.

978-0-7387-1262-8 • 6 x 9, 360 pp. • $18.95

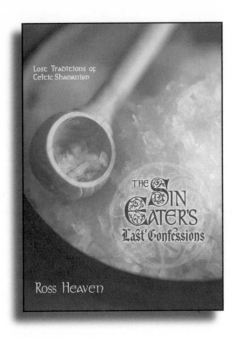

Lost Traditions of
Celtic Shamanism

THE SIN
EATER'S
Last Confessions

Ross Heaven

The Sin Eater's Last Confessions
Lost Traditions of Celtic Shamanism

Ross Heaven

Considered a madman in his English village, Adam Dilwyn Vaughan—a sin eater—was shunned by the same community who flocked to him for healing. This true tale records Ross Heaven's fascinating journey as the sin eater's apprentice, who is introduced to the lost art of sin eating and other Celtic shamanic traditions.

This spiritual memoir records the author's wondrous, moving experiences with the powerful energies of the natural world. He witnesses Adam removing negative energies from a patient, discovers his soul purpose through dreaming, goes on a vision quest in a sacred cave, and participates in a sin-eating ritual. Interlacing these remarkable events are Welsh legends and enlightening discussions that shed light on these mysterious practices and invite you to see the world through the eyes of a shaman. Also included is a sin eater's workbook of the same shamanic exercises and techniques practiced by Adam.

978-0-7387-1356-4 • 5 x 7, 288 pp. • bibliog., index • $16.95

To Write to the Author

If you wish to contact the author or would like more information about this book, please write to the author in care of Llewellyn Worldwide and we will forward your request. Both the author and the publisher appreciate hearing from you and learning of your enjoyment of this book and how it has helped you. Llewellyn Worldwide cannot guarantee that every letter written to the author can be answered, but all will be forwarded. Please write to:

Ellen Evert Hopman
^c/o Llewellyn Worldwide
2143 Wooddale Drive
Woodbury, MN 55125-2989

Please enclose a self-addressed stamped envelope for reply,
or $1.00 to cover costs. If outside U.S.A., enclose
international postal reply coupon.

Many of Llewellyn's authors have websites with additional information and resources. For more information, please visit our website:

http://www.llewellyn.com